# THE OPENING YOUR HEART SERIES

**Beloved:** *Opening Your Heart, Part I,* is a six-lesson Bible study that lays a strong foundation for our true identity as beloved daughters of God.

**Unshaken:** *Opening Your Heart, Part II,* is a six-lesson Bible study that fills our spiritual toolbox with exactly what we need to grow stronger in our faith.

**Steadfast:** *Opening Your Heart, Part III,* a six-lesson Bible study, unpacks why we are hustling for our worth and how to conquer our fears.

## THE KEEPING IN BALANCE SERIES

*Harmony: Keeping in Balance, Part I*
*Perspective: Keeping in Balance, Part II*
*Exhale: Keeping in Balance, Part III*

## THE DISCOVERING OUR DIGNITY SERIES

*Tapestry: Discovering Our Dignity, Part I*
*Legacy: Discovering our Dignity, Part II*
*Heritage: Discovering Our Dignity, Part III*

For more information on all Walking with Purpose Bible studies please visit us at
**walkingwithpurpose.com**

walking with purpose

## walking with purpose

Dear Friend,

Welcome to *Beloved,* part I of the *Opening Your Heart* young adult Bible study series! You are about to begin an exciting journey closer to the heart of God. You can come as you are—with your questions, doubts, joys, and hopes.

If you are doing this study with a group of friends, I am praying that you'll find it to be a safe place to let down your guard. I'm asking God to surround you with young women who want to encourage you and walk alongside you as you all explore the basics of our faith. No question is dumb, and no confidence should be shared outside the group, so masks can be dropped at the door. This is a place where you get to be real. My hope is that instead of comparison and competition, you'll find community. You weren't meant to go it alone.

How I wish I could be sitting with you, hearing your thoughts and insights about all the things we're going to delve into during this study. Your generation is setting the world on fire as you seek to live authentically, desire to spend your money in a way that makes a positive social impact, and step out to restore what's broken in our culture. You are trailblazers, hope igniters, and grace givers. When you lead with love and point to Christ, hearts engage and are changed.

But you can only share with others what you have first received. And what I desire most for you is that you will receive the truth that you belong, that you are relentlessly loved, that you have a calling and a purpose, and that nothing in your life is a waste. I want you to know who you are *in Christ,* and the difference He makes. You can stand strong, no matter what life blows your way, if you stay rooted in these truths.

Being grounded in truth means that you have got to saturate your mind and heart with Scripture. Without that foundation, you'll have difficulty recognizing God's voice—deciphering truth from lies. The Bible is a far better anchor than your emotions or circumstances. So join me as we dive into God's Word, inviting Jesus to intersect and transform our daily lives.

With prayers for you as you open your heart to the One who loves you best ~

Love,
*Lisa Brenninkmeyer*
*Founder and Chief Purpose Officer, Walking with Purpose*

# Beloved
*Opening Your Heart* Series
Part I

www.walkingwithpurpose.com

Authored by Lisa Brenninkmeyer
Cover and page design by True Cotton
Production management by Christine Welsko

**IMPRIMATUR**     + William E. Lori, S.T.D., Archbishop of Baltimore

Printed: November 2017

ISBN: 978-1-943173-11-2

Beloved: *Opening Your Heart* Series, Part I

# TABLE OF CONTENTS

## INTRODUCTION

## LESSONS

## APPENDICES

## ANSWER KEY

## PRAYER PAGES

# Welcome to Walking with Purpose

You have many choices when it comes to how you spend your time—thank you for choosing Walking with Purpose. Studying God's Word with an open and receptive heart will bring spiritual growth and enrichment to all aspects of your life, making every moment that you've invested well worth it.

Each one of us comes to this material from our own unique vantage point. You are welcome as you are. No previous experience is necessary. Some of you will find that the questions in this study cause you to think about concepts that are new to you. Others might find much is a review. God meets each one of us where we are, and He is always faithful, taking us to a deeper, better place spiritually, regardless of where we begin.

## The Structure of *Opening Your Heart* Series

The *Opening Your Heart* series is a three-part Bible study, each of which can stand alone, or all three can be completed one after the other. Each six-week Bible study integrates Scripture with the teachings of the Roman Catholic Church to point us to principles that help us manage life's pace and pressure while living with calm and steadiness.

This Bible study can be used on your own, giving you great material for daily Scripture meditation and prayer. It also lends itself well to group discussion. We encourage you to gather your tribe—a handful of friends who want more out of their spiritual lives. The accountability and deeper friendship that will result make it so much easier to live out the truths contained in these pages.

## Study Guide Format and Reference Materials

The three parts of *Opening Your Heart* is divided into three sections:

The first section comprises six lessons, which are divided into five "days" to help you form a habit of reading and reflecting on God's Word regularly. If you are a young woman who has only bits and pieces of time throughout your day to accomplish tasks, you will find this breakdown of the lessons especially helpful. Each day focuses on Scripture readings and related teaching passages, and ends with a Quiet Your Heart reflection, which should lead you to a time of personal prayer. In addition, Day Five includes a Saint's Story; a lesson conclusion; a resolution section, in which you set a goal for yourself based on a theme of the lesson; and short clips from the *Catechism of the Catholic Church*, which are referenced throughout the lesson to complement the Scripture study.

The second section, the appendices, contains supplemental materials referred to during the study.

The third section contains the answer key. You will benefit so much more from the course study if you work through the questions on your own, searching your heart, as this is your very personal journey of faith. The answer key is meant to enhance small group discussion and provide personal guidance or insight when needed.

A memory verse has been chosen for each part of the *Opening Your Heart*, and we encourage you to memorize each of them as you move through the course. An illustration of the Bible verse can be found at the back of the Bible study, and color versions and phone lock screens can be downloaded from our website.

At the end of the book are pages on which to write weekly prayer intentions.

**The Bible**
The recommended Bible translations for use in Walking with Purpose studies are: The New American Bible, which is the translation used in the United States for the readings at Mass; The Revised Standard Version, Catholic Edition; and The Jerusalem Bible.

# Walking with Purpose™ Young Adult Bible Studies

## The *Opening Your Heart* Series

***Beloved:*** *Opening Your Heart, Part I* is a six-lesson Bible study that lays a strong foundation for our true identity as beloved daughters of God. We'll learn that we belong to a family that will never abandon us. We'll encounter grace and practical tools to make God our first priority. Jesus will meet us personally in the pages of His Word, and we'll be transformed as a result.

***Unshaken:*** *Opening Your Heart, Part II* is a six-lesson Bible study that fills our spiritual toolbox with exactly what we need to grow stronger in our faith. We'll discuss why and how we should read the Bible, what difference the sacraments really make in our lives, how to bravely face challenges in our efforts to follow Christ, and the way Mary perfectly mothers us through it all.

***Steadfast:*** *Opening Your Heart, Part III,* a six-lesson Bible study, unpacks why we are hustling for our worth and how to conquer our fears. We'll look at the role of suffering and forgiveness in our lives, and dig deeper into how we can truly change in the areas where we have felt enslaved. We'll explore life purpose, our vocations, and the depth of God's personal love for His beloved children.

## The *Keeping in Balance* Series: *Coming Soon*

***Harmony:*** *Keeping in Balance, Part I* is a seven-lesson Bible study that helps us to get a grip on our lives by looking at the importance of authenticity, setting priorities, managing expectations, and having healthy relationships. We'll also explore finding a balance between mediocrity and perfectionism so that we can become the women God created us to be without stressing or striving.

***Perspective:*** *Keeping in Balance, Part II* is a six-lesson Bible study that addresses how we can become more content, grow stronger in areas where we've failed a million times, and get moving when we feel like settling for the status quo. *Perspective* also explores how we can engage our culture as Catholics at a time when the reputation of Christians is at an all-time low.

***Exhale:*** *Keeping in Balance, Part III* is a six-lesson Bible study that helps us establish a rhythm of rest, worship, and surrender. If you long for more simplicity in your life and are ready to order your thoughts so you can experience inner peace, this Bible study will both inspire you and provide you with practical steps to make positive changes.

# The *Discovering Our Dignity* Series: *Coming Soon*

**Tapestry:** *Discovering Our Dignity, Part I* is a six-lesson Bible study that explores the beginning of salvation history through the eyes of the women of Genesis. The difficulties they struggled with are remarkably similar to our own: relationship challenges, the death of dreams, the lure of compromise, and the danger of self-reliance. We'll learn from their mistakes as we apply age-old wisdom to our modern challenges.

**Legacy:** *Discovering Our Dignity, Part II* is a nine-lesson Bible study that picks up where *Tapestry* left off. Our exploration of the women of salvation history continues as we move further into the Old Testament. We'll explore a myriad of women's issues such as loneliness, shame, leadership challenges, and making a difference in the world.

**Heritage:** *Discovering Our Dignity, Part III* is a seven-lesson Bible Study that highlights key women of the New Testament. Mary and Martha will help us explore the balance of work and worship, and the poor widow will shed new light on what it means to live sacrificially. We'll be inspired especially by Mary, the Blessed Mother, as we apply her wisdom to our daily challenges.

# Walking with Purpose™ Website

Please visit our website at www.walkingwithpurpose.com to find supplemental materials that complement our Bible studies; a link to our online store for additional Bible studies, DVDs, books, and more; and the following free content:

***WWP Scripture Printables*** of our exclusively designed verse cards that complement all Bible studies. Available in various sizes, lock screens for phones, and a format that allows you to e-mail them to friends.

***WWP Bible Study Playlists*** of Lisa's favorite music to accompany each Bible study.

***WWP Videos*** of all Connect Coffee Talks by Lisa Brenninkmeyer.

***WWP Blog by Lisa Brenninkmeyer,*** a safe place where you are welcome, where the mask can drop and you can be real. Subscribe for updates.

### WWP Leadership Development Program

We are here to help you take your leadership to the next level! Through our training, you'll discover insights that help you achieve your leadership potential. You'll be empowered to step out of your comfort zone and experience the rush of serving God with passion and purpose. We want you to know that you are not alone; we offer you encouragement and the tools you need to reach out to a world that desperately needs to experience the love of God.

### Links to WWP Social Media

Twitter, Pinterest, Facebook, Instagram

# Walking with Purpose™ Mission Statement

Walking with Purpose aims to bring women to a deeper personal relationship with Jesus Christ by offering personal studies and small group discussions that link our everyday challenges and struggles with the solutions given to us through the teachings of Christ and the Roman Catholic Church.

## About the Author

Lisa Brenninkmeyer, raised as an evangelical Protestant, entered the Catholic Church in 1991. She has led Bible studies in Europe, Mexico, and the United States, and has written curricula for women and children. She founded Walking with Purpose in 2008 out of a desire to see women come to know Christ personally. Her speaking and writing are inspired by a desire to see women transformed as they realize how much God loves them. She holds a BA in psychology from St. Olaf College. She lives with her husband, Leo, and their seven children in St. Augustine, Florida.

# Lessons

Walking with Purpose is a community of women growing in faith – together! This is where women are gathering. Join us!

www.walkingwithpurpose.com/find-program-near

# Lesson 1

# ABBA ~ GOD THE FATHER

## Introduction

*"How great is the love the Father has lavished on us that we should be called children of God!"* *(1 John 3:1)*

You are the daughter of a generous, protective, and engaged Father, a Father who will never leave you or abandon you.

And for many of us, this is one of the hardest things in the world to truly believe.

A lot of things get in the way of us taking that truth deep into our hearts. Perhaps your own father failed to love you well, and that has messed with how you see your heavenly Father. Your life experiences might contain enough suffering that you have trouble trusting a Father who didn't appear to care for or protect you. Or maybe your block comes from something you have done, something that makes you feel disqualified to bear the label "beloved daughter of God."

In Matthew 7:9–10, Jesus asks, "Which one of you would hand his son a stone when he asks for a loaf of bread, or a snake when he asks for a fish?" And then He goes on to say, "If you then, who are wicked, know how to give good gifts to your children, how much more will your heavenly Father give good things to those who ask him" (Matthew 7:11). The point He is making is that if imperfect earthly fathers (at least ones who aren't cruel or somehow unable) give their children what they need, we can count on our heavenly Father to give us good things—as opposed to holding out on us—if we ask Him.

What makes it so hard for us to believe this? It's not just our personal experiences; it's also the result of what happened all those years ago in the Garden of Eden. That's the first place where the seed of doubt regarding the Father's goodness was planted in the human heart. God had surrounded Adam and Eve with beauty, abundance, and provision. Only one thing was withheld, the fruit from the tree of the knowledge of good and evil. When the serpent slithered up to Eve, he asked her, "Did God really say, You shall not eat from any of the trees in the garden?" Look at him, making God's restriction sound even worse. See how the liar exaggerated in order to make his point? And Eve paused, and engaged with the enemy. She leaned in and listened to the father of lies (John 8:44), and added to God's words. Instead of just saying that they weren't to eat the fruit, she said that they weren't to touch it either. The truth about God's words became fuzzy, and the slide toward compromise and slavery to sin began.

In this lesson, we are going to look at some of the characteristics of God the Father. But before we begin, I'd like us to try to clear our minds and hearts of the thoughts that will tempt us to doubt His goodness. I want to challenge you to decide, here and now, that you are done listening to lies. I encourage you to take a leap of faith—a step toward believing that God the Father loves you and is treating you as a good father should—by praying the following:

Dear Lord,

I'm done listening to lies. I may not understand why you have allowed certain things into my life and withheld others, but one thing I do know: I want my mind to be filled with truth. So I ask you, Jesus, what is the lie that I am believing about the Father? [Pause, and pay attention to what comes to mind. Then take the first lie that comes into your mind and say:] Jesus, will you take that lie from me forever? Father, what's the truth? Show me who you really are. Amen.

I encourage you to repeat that prayer each morning. May Jesus reveal to you that "You did not receive a spirit of slavery to fall back into fear, but you received a spirit of adoption, through which we cry, 'Abba, Father!'" (Romans 8:15). "So you are no longer a slave but a child, and if a child then also an heir, through God" (Galatians 4:7).

Let's delve into God's Word together, and get to know our Abba . . . our Papa . . . our Father.

# Day One
# YOUR HEAVENLY FATHER DELIGHTS IN YOU

God the Father is completely captivated by you. He loves you. When His eyes scan the crowd and catch sight of you, He lights up with pride and says, "There's my girl." Do you find that hard to believe? Circumstances in your past and present can make it difficult to grasp this truth, but here's the thing: Something can *be* true even when it doesn't *feel* true. Because of this, two things need to happen for us to begin understanding the heart of our heavenly Father:

First, we need to take the time to get to know God the Father better, *as He has revealed Himself in Scripture*. We get ourselves into trouble when we try to figure things out based simply on what we currently have in our minds and how things appear to be in the moment. The Bible is the best place to start if we are having trouble understanding who God is. It's in His own words. It's His own witness. This is exactly what you're doing right now, so you're on the right track.

Second, we need to stop judging God by our circumstances, and start judging our circumstances by a bigger view of God. All too often, we look at the things we have that we don't want and the things we want but don't have, and conclude that God is holding out on us or doesn't care. That's what results when we judge God by our circumstances. When we develop a bigger, wider-angled view of God, we see that there is more to our circumstances, sufferings, and limitations than meets the eye. God is at work, even when we don't see evidence of it.

1. What insight does Isaiah 55:8–9 offer as we wrestle with circumstances that we don't like or understand?




2. What do the following verses tell you about how God sees you?

   Isaiah 43:4 (the first part of the verse)


   Psalm 139:13–4


   2 Corinthians 5:17

Jeremiah 31:3

Psalm 118:6

Zephaniah 3:17

3. It can be hard to believe that you have a heavenly Father who delights in you, especially if you have been basing whether this is true on how pleasant your current circumstances are. Another thing that can get in the way of opening up to the love of God the Father is awareness of all the ways we have messed up. We look at our behavior and wonder if we're beyond the reach of God's mercy. We might feel we've failed one time too many or that what we've done is just too awful to be forgiven. What do the following verses tell us about how God sees our sin?

Psalm 103:12

Isaiah 1:18

1 John 1:9

You have probably been told that God forgives sin, but there's something powerful about hearing it in His own words. If you find it hard to forgive yourself, go back to these verses and remember that God does not lie. Your past sin does not define you. You have been given a fresh start.

4. Do you find it hard to believe that God delights in you? Is something standing in the way of you embracing God the Father's unconditional love for you?

*Quiet your heart and enjoy His presence. . . . God delights in you unwaveringly.*

*A Brazilian pastor told the story of a young widow whose beautiful teenage daughter dreamed day and night about moving from their small town to the big city of Rio de Janeiro. Her mother tried to warn her that the city could be a dangerous place. Jobs were scarce and life could be cruel. But her daughter was independent and determined. The mother knew what the girl might have to do to make a living if she went to the big city and couldn't find work. That's why she was heartbroken to awaken one morning to find only a note telling her that her daughter was gone.*

*The mother hurriedly packed a bag and headed for the bus station to follow the girl to Rio. On the way to the bus, she stopped at a drugstore and sat in one of those booths where you can put quarters in and take photographs of yourself. She arrived in Rio with her purse full of those little photos. She went everyplace she thought she might find her daughter, but without any success. Fearing the worst, she began to check all the bars, hotels, and nightclubs with a reputation for streetwalkers and prostitutes. And everywhere she went, she left one of her photos taped on a bathroom mirror, tacked on a hotel bulletin board, stuck in the corner of a phone booth. On the back of each photo, she wrote a note to her daughter. It wasn't long before both her pictures and her money ran out and she had to return home, feeling that she had failed.*

*A few weeks later, in one of those dumpy hotels, her daughter started down the stairs. Her eyes no longer sparkled; her young face was tired. Her dream had become a nightmare. Yet she knew there was no way she could ever go home again. At the bottom of the stairs, her eye caught one of those familiar photographs taped to the lobby mirror. Removing it, she found the note on the back: "Whatever you have done, whatever you've become, it doesn't matter. Please come home." She did.*[1]

*Some of you may need to hear those words from Christ today. "Whatever you have done, whatever you've become, it doesn't matter. Please come home and discover God's love for you. You are His delight."*


# Day Two
# YOUR HEAVENLY FATHER DEFENDS YOU

*"He found them in a wilderness, a wasteland of howling desert. He shielded them, cared for them, guarded them as the apple of his eye." (Deuteronomy 32:10)*

---

[1] Max Lucado, *No Wonder They Call Him the Savior* (Nashville, TN: Thomas Nelson, 2004), 129–31.

It's dark and frightening in the wilderness. The wasteland makes everything seem pointless and can cause us to feel ruined. When we're in the howling desert, searching for an oasis, our desperation can reach a fever pitch.

This is where our Father meets us. We are lost and wandering, and He comes for us. Instead of waiting for us to clean up and make our way back to Him, He goes on a rescue mission, enters into the confusion and the mess, and grabs hold of His daughters. As we're promised in Matthew 18:14, "Your Father in heaven is not willing that any one of these little ones should be lost." That includes you. He has come to rescue you, the apple of His eye.

1. When we feel like God is slow to bring the relief we desire, is it fair to assume that He is asleep on the job? See Psalm 121:1–8 and note the ways in which God is looking after you.

2. A. Our limited perspective means the struggle we are in the midst of isn't always what it appears to be on the surface. God has the big picture, seeing things invisible to us. What insight do we gain from Ephesians 6:12 in terms of many of the challenges we face?

God defends us in the spiritual battle. Although this battlefield can be invisible to the naked eye, it's no less perilous. God defends us in places where we can't even see what is truly going on.

B. We have an enemy who is behind all the hits we take on the spiritual battlefield. How is this enemy described in CCC 2851?

C. What does God promise when our enemy, the devil, uses weapons against His beloved daughters? See Isaiah 54:17.

The enemy may think he has fashioned the perfect weapon to take you out at the knees. We know from St. Ignatius' Discernment of Spirits that the enemy makes a study of our souls and attacks where we are weakest. But an amazing thing happens when he pulls out his weapon and strikes the apple of God's eye: God takes that very weapon and turns it back on the enemy. How does He do that? By allowing the attack to alert His beloved daughters to an area of weakness or woundedness that God wants to strengthen and heal. Suffering brings all sorts of long-buried things to the surface. Sometimes it's the only way God can get to those deep places in our hearts to set us free. What Satan intends to use to destroy us, God uses to transform us in beautiful ways—if we cooperate with the process.

3. What perspective can be found in 2 Corinthians 4:8–9 when we feel as if we are being devastated by the battles in life?

You may feel like God isn't defending you the way you'd like, but you have *not* been destroyed. You are still here. You are still standing. You may be hard-pressed on every side, but you are not crushed. You may be perplexed, but God can hold you back from despair. You may feel the heat of persecution, but you are never forsaken. You may be struck down, flat on the mat, but you are not destroyed.

4. In what area of your life are you feeling powerless or helpless? Write a prayer below, telling God how you are feeling. Don't hold back. He wants you to bring your whole heart to Him, not some edited version. He isn't afraid of or overwhelmed by your emotions. Then ask God for His protection. Invite Him into that place of powerlessness and ask Him to show up and defend you. I promise you, *He will do it*. It may not be in the way that you expect. You might want to ask Him for supernatural insight so you can see the ways in which He is taking the weapons intended to harm you and transforming them into blessings.

Dear God,

"The Lord will fight for you; you have only to keep still." (Exodus 14:14)

*Quiet your heart and enjoy His presence. . . . He is your fortress and your shield.*

*"The Lord is good, a stronghold in the day of trouble; and He knows those who trust in Him." (Nahum 1:7)*

*In the time when the Bible was written, a stronghold was a fortified building that offered the greatest structural protection in an area. People ran to it in the midst of battle and hid there.*

*All too often, when the battle rages around us, we construct our own strongholds. They might seem to offer protection, but ultimately, they always disappoint. We might build a stronghold of perfectionism ("If I do everything perfectly, I'll be OK"), or addiction ("If I can just have one more [x], I'll feel that I can cope"), or shopping ("Amazon Prime will take the edge off"), or Netflix ("I need to numb out"). Man-made strongholds never deliver on their promises. The only stronghold that we can count on no matter what isn't a thing; it's a person. It's God. He is our stronghold in the day of trouble. And He is good.*

*Where are you running? Where do you hide when it all seems too much? Could it be that there is a better place to go? Run to God and "He will shelter you with his [feathers], and under his wings you may take refuge; his faithfulness is a protecting shield" (Psalm 91:4). Ask Him to be your safeguard and your fortress, your stronghold, your deliverer, your shield, your refuge (Psalm 144:1–2). He will never refuse this prayer.*

## Day Three
# YOUR HEAVENLY FATHER DISCIPLINES YOU

What is the first thing most of us do when we get on a roller coaster ride? We test the safety bar to make sure it truly is working. What's going through our minds when we test it? Do we want to find that it has some give and isn't a firm barrier? Absolutely not. We push on it in hopes that it'll hold fast because we want assurance that we're not going to fall out when we're hanging upside down.

Life without boundaries and guidelines from God would be a bit like careening through an amusement park ride without the safety barrier in place. We need to know what is safe and what isn't, and because of our tendency to test the boundaries, we need discipline to help us to stay within the lanes. Whether we like it or not, consequences help us to learn.

The passage we're going to unpack today is a tough one. Most people choose not to study this passage in Hebrews, because it isn't a feel-good chapter. It's confusing, leaving us with *some* understanding, but a lot of mystery, too. Most young adults who choose to lean into these verses have experienced suffering. If you have experienced some significant trials, the truths contained here could change your perspective. Maybe. It all depends on whether you choose to believe what you read and determine to trust in God's goodness. A leap of faith is required, because God never promises to answer each and every question we ask. But He does promise to be loving and faithful. Will we take Him at His word, even when we don't understand?

**Read Hebrews 12:5–11.**

1. A. According to Hebrews 12:5–6, whom does the Lord discipline?



   B. According to Hebrews 12:7, what are we to endure as "discipline"?

C. According to Hebrews 12:10, in what way does God want His discipline to benefit us?

Sometimes discipline is obviously the consequence of our poor choices. We mess up and later pay the price. We may not like it, but at least we know what's going on. But when God's discipline comes in the form of trials, we often feel confused. We want Him to give an explanation for what He is allowing, and more often than not, He seems silent. So we begin to wrestle.

We wrestle with whether God really is in control. Because if He is, and if He loves us, then why won't He make the painful trial end? Seasons of suffering can leave us with all sorts of questions, and we run the risk of losing heart.

What this passage is telling us is that the very things people intend to use to hurt us, God wants to use to discipline us—to teach, correct, transform, and heal us. There is not an ounce of suffering that is not without meaning or purpose, if we will allow God to work on our hearts through it.

When we are going through trials, God is not a passive observer. Nor is He unable to intervene, bringing good from the situation only later, as a way to redeem at least some aspect of it. God is all-powerful and in control, and He's at work. But our cooperation is required.

2. According to Hebrews 12:11, discipline brings "the peaceful fruit of righteousness" to whom?

God's discipline bears fruit in the lives of women who are teachable. These are women who are asking the right question. Instead of saying, "Why is this happening to me?" these women ask, "What can I learn from this?"

In no way is this easy. Those who ask this question often do so through tears and brokenness. But the one truth they will not let go of is that somehow, in the midst of this pain and agony, God is still good. Instead of judging God by their circumstances, they assess their circumstances through lenses that focus on His steadfast love.

3. What difficult circumstances are you facing currently? Are you able to ask God, "What can I learn from this?" Can you look to the past and find an example of a time when God transformed you through the discipline of trials?

4. The Old Testament is filled with examples of God disciplining His children out of love for them, while teaching them how to behave like beloved sons and daughters. Moses had a front row seat to many of those lessons. During one of the most significant episodes of discipline, after the Israelites had worshipped the golden calf, God revealed His character to Moses in Exodus 34:6–7. Read the verses, and record what it says about God the Father.

What a passage. The first part brings us comfort. We love to read about God's graciousness and mercy. We wipe our brow in relief when we read that He is slow to anger, abounding in love, and lavish in offering forgiveness. But then we read of punishment being passed down to the children—to the fourth generation—and we cry foul. What is going on here? What we might see as God cursing an unborn and unsuspecting generation is better understood as the way natural consequences are felt. When a parent makes destructive choices—say, with alcoholism or any kind of abuse—the consequences continue to be felt for subsequent generations. Patterns of behavior are established. Behaviors are modeled, protected, and all too often passed down and emulated.

But those sinful patterns of behavior do not have the last word among people who choose to be transformed by their trials. There are brave women who stop saying, "This isn't fair" (although there is no doubt about it, it is not fair). Instead, they say, "This pattern stops now and healing begins here." When God is invited into the process, everything can change. We do not need to end as we have begun.

21

*Quiet your heart and enjoy His presence. . . . Our sufferings "are as nothing compared with the glory to be revealed" (Romans 8:18).*

*"For momentary, light affliction is producing for us an eternal weight of glory far beyond all comparison, while we look not at the things which are seen, but at the things which are not seen; for the things which are seen are temporal, but the things which are not seen are eternal." (2 Corinthians 4:17–18)*

*God keeps His eyes on the big picture. His discipline is always for the purpose of "producing for us an eternal weight of glory." It may be temporarily painful. But to those who are willing to learn the lessons and be transformed by the pain, there is something better, richer, more satisfying on the other side.*

*What we must never lose sight of is God's motivation. He disciplines us because He loves us, not because He hates us. His discipline is not His anger; it is His fatherly protection and instruction. Rarely will we understand His ways and methods. More often than not, His timetable will be slower than ours. But for those who wait, for those who are humble enough to be taught, for those who cling to His steadfast love, something glorious and beyond our imaginings will come.*

*"Wait for the Lord; be strong, and take heart." (Psalm 27:14)*

## Day Four
# YOUR HEAVENLY FATHER DREAMS WITH YOU

Nestled within your soul is the potential to change the world. You have gifts that the world desperately needs, a voice that matters, a beauty to reveal. All the things you see in the world that make you cry out for grace and justice? God the Father watches your heart enflame, and waits to see if you will answer His call. As it turns out, He cares about those deep, wild, impossible dreams, and He is calling you forth to explore them with Him.

1. What do you learn from Jeremiah 29:11 about God's plan for your life?

You were not created for some stale, safe, generic existence. You were created to reflect God's love to a world that desperately needs to see that He is real, He is good, and He cares for us all. This brings Him glory and is why we are here. There is nothing more thrilling than letting God weave your soul, your story, your dreams, and His desires into a tapestry of His design.

It would all be so amazing if it weren't for the waiting.

Waiting to see exactly what that tapestry is going to look like can just about do you in. Will the story include the guy of your dreams? If it does, when is he going to show up? Or is that even what you're supposed to be pursuing? Are you called to the religious life? What does your future hold? You want answers. You want it all laid out. And God cups your face in His loving hands and whispers, "Trust me."

So how do we remain dreamers and trusters at the same time?

2. The following verses can act as a litmus test for our dreams. Read each one and record any insights.

   Matthew 6:33

If we are seeking to build up the kingdom of God, that means we aren't trying to build up our own at the same time; instead, we take a look at the motives behind our dreams. Are you seeking a platform? Will you mind if others get the glory, not you?

Philippians 2:3–4

Checking our motives is not a box that we check one time–never having to return to the task again. The truth is, self-centeredness and ambition can infiltrate a dream that was once quite pure in motive. If we are willing to examine why we do what we do regularly, God has the chance to speak to our hearts and draw us back to the right intentions. When the waters get muddied by our self-focus, that doesn't mean we have to quit. But it does mean we need to purify our hearts and get back on track.

Another good question to ask ourselves is if our dream is in the interests of others. Do others benefit if the dream comes true, or do we?

3. The following verses give us insight into what it means to trust. Read them and apply them to the trust required in patiently waiting.

Proverbs 3:5–6

Proverbs 28:26

Walking in wisdom isn't something that just automatically happens. Wisdom is the ability to take the things you know to be true and apply them to real-life situations. It means taking the time to learn what God says, and then relying on those truths in day-to-day life. The alternative is assuming that we know better—that we already know enough.

I can remember a time in my early twenties when I felt completely stuck and sidelined. I was living in Germany and had no work permit; the only job I was allowed to do was babysitting or teaching English. Neither option sounded good to me. I remember calling my dad and telling him it all felt like such a waste. I had dreams of teaching, or speaking, or writing, but there weren't any open doors in front of me. My dad challenged me to take that time as a gift—a chance to grow in wisdom, to dig deep into Scripture and study so that when an opportunity came, I would actually have something to say. Those words were game changing for me. Some of my richest studying of the Bible and memorization of Scripture came out of those years that felt wasted. I still go back to old notes and know without a doubt that a foundation of God's wisdom was laid in my heart in those years.

The truth is, you can achieve things beyond your wildest dreams. I pray you would dream big and bold. But I also pray that while waiting and trusting, you would find someone to *serve* and give it your all. I pray you would give to this person out of the abundant gifts that God has placed in you. And I pray that instead of quitting when it isn't fun anymore, you would push through. That you would show grit. I pray you would give everything you have and make the most of where you are today. Be faithful where you are, and God will see to the results.

Isaiah 43:1

This verse bears special significance for those who are waiting for the right guy to come along. It's always a temptation to look to a man to fill what's empty in your heart and to affirm your worth. But when we pursue a relationship with those expectations, we will always be disappointed. The starting point always needs to be that God says, "You are mine." We need to grab hold of that promise and lean into it. We need to mine it for all the truth it contains. No man will ever be to us what God can be.

4. What are you dreaming about? When you run your dreams through the litmus test of the Scriptures in this lesson, do you gain any insights? In what ways can you use the time in front of you to become better prepared for future opportunities?

*Quiet your heart and enjoy His presence. . . . Your gifts and dreams can build up the body of Christ.*

*"Every dream or desire you have that comes from God is an invitation for more intimacy with Him."*
*—Holley Gerth*

*God created you with a purpose. Your purpose—your calling—is unique. That means you won't discover it by comparing yourself with your girlfriends or your sister. He has called you to run a race and keep your eye on your own lane. Figuring out which race that is—what your specific calling is— is a messy process. It's always a matter of getting to know God better, looking at the ways in which your suffering can be a bridge to others, exploring the things that make you feel fully alive, and being alert to the needs around you.*

*The great thing about God is that He steers a moving ship. He doesn't wait until you have every detail sorted out before letting you set sail. You'll learn as much from your failures as you will from your successes.*

*Please don't settle for playing it safe. Remember the words of Pope Benedict XVI: "The world promises you comfort, but you were not made for comfort. You were made for greatness." And please don't sit on your gifts, dreams, and hopes because you're afraid that if you step out you'll be criticized or you'll be too much or too little. Don't be afraid to dream. God's perfect love casts out fear (1 John 4:18). He is the wind behind you, urging you to go for it. He will catch you if you fall, dust you off, and encourage you to set out again. There are things in the world that break His heart. Do they break yours? Then grab hold of His hand and set out to make a difference. Your voice, your dream, your heart are so needed.*

# Day Five
# SAINT'S STORY

## Saint Thérèse of Lisieux

Have you ever had any of these thoughts?

I'm tired of failing—over and over again. I'm sure God is sick of me. He must be getting tired of the fact that I keep making the same mistakes, over and over. His forgiveness must reach a limit. What God has asked of me is just too much. I can't do it. The obedient Christian life must not be for me. I want to give up. I am spiritually weary. I don't know how to share my faith; I can barely live it myself.

When this is how we are feeling, the teachings of Saint Thérèse of Lisieux can offer us tremendous comfort and encouragement. The simplicity of the faith that she lays out for us is so completely *Catholic* that Pope Pius XII said, "She rediscovered the Gospel itself, the very heart of the Gospel."[2]

If he is saying that she "rediscovered" it, then something had been lost in the way our faith was being communicated. We can still see evidence of this today when we feel unnecessarily burdened by a legalism that does not reflect the gospel of grace.

When Saint Thérèse's book, *The Story of a Soul*, became available, the truths contained in it were like a healing balm for people who had become afraid of God. Many had allowed their impression of God's standard of holiness to turn Him into a tyrant who lacked mercy—someone who was just waiting for people to mess up so He could swoop down and condemn them. Saint Thérèse's words pointed to a simpler approach to the spiritual life: a childlike faith that pleases God enormously.

This was the faith that Saint Thérèse had in abundance. She responded to God's love with love, like a child naturally does when she knows she is adored and cherished. Her confidence that her heavenly Father could accomplish what she was unable to allowed her to rest in His arms in a childlike surrender—the perfect posture of trust.

Her faith was childlike, but it was not childish. A childish faith is rooted in unrealistic expectations. "It's not fair!" the child screams. In contrast, childlike faith leaves room for limitless possibilities. Children believe in unicorns, magic, and Santa making it down every chimney across the globe in one night. Unencumbered by preconceived notions, they think anything is possible.

---

[2] Father Jean C. J. d'Elbee, *I Believe in Love* (Manchester, NH: Sophia Institute Press, 2001), 3.

Think of the way we limit God with the things we figure He would never do. Having childlike faith means doing things like lowering a paralytic through a ceiling to Jesus or reaching out to touch just the hem of Jesus' garment in hopes of being healed.

Saint Thérèse was able to abandon herself to God because she figured He could do anything. Like most little girls, she wanted to be the princess in a fairy tale. She wanted to be romanced by her knight in shining armor. She figured out at a far younger age than most of us that there is no one who rescues quite like her heavenly Father.

She was a dreamer and a truster. There's no question that she went after what she wanted. Not many other young women would have made their way to Rome to beg the Holy Father to allow them to enter the convent early, but Saint Thérèse did. Even after being told that she was forbidden to speak to the pope, that it would take too long, she ran forward and knelt at his feet, making her request with tear-filled eyes. When the pope told her to do whatever the superiors said, which was to wait, she didn't give up. Her dogged determination, tenacity, and prayer made all the difference, and she was allowed to enter early. She dreamed, she pursued, and she trusted God to make it all happen—which He did. When our passions are ultimately about God, our hearts are free to dream the impossible.

**When have you seen evidence of child*ish* faith in your own life? When have you seen evidence of the child*like* faith of Saint Thérèse?**


## Conclusion

*"We aren't meant to figure life out on our own. God wants to father us. The truth is, he has been fathering us for a long time—we just haven't had the eyes to see it. He wants to father us much more intimately, but we have to be in a posture to receive it."*[3] —*John Eldredge*

What kind of a posture helps us to receive God's fatherly care? It's a posture of humility, openness, and receptivity. The prophet Isaiah reflected this perfectly when he said, "O Lord, you are our Father. We are the clay, you the potter; we are the work of your hands" (Isaiah 64:8).

God the Father is trying to coax us into His lap, where we can rest. He is longing to gaze into our eyes and speak our true identity into our hearts. If we would stop

---

[3] John Eldredge, *Fathered by God* (Nashville, TN: Thomas Nelson, 2009), 11.

thrashing around, trying to be the ones in control and in charge, we would be better able to hear His voice.

God comes to us with the same question He posed to Adam and Eve when they were hiding in the garden: "Where are you?" (Genesis 3:9).

All too often, the place He finds me is on the stage, performing my heart out. I'm not resting in His lap, because I am too busy trying to earn His approval. I'm like a performing orphan, wanting to be chosen, hoping to be considered good enough. And this breaks my heavenly Father's heart, because I am trying to earn something that I already have.

He has chosen you and me already. It wasn't based on anything we did, but it has everything to do with what Jesus did on our behalf. We'll start to explore this in the next lessons. As we transition to a focus on Jesus, we will still be learning about God the Father, because in Jesus' own words, "Anyone who has seen me has seen the Father. . . . The words I say to you are not just my own. Rather, it is the Father, living in me, who is doing his work" (John 14:9–10).

## My Resolution

**In what specific way will I apply what I have learned in this lesson?**

"My Resolution" is your opportunity to write down one specific personal application from this lesson. We can take in a lot of information from studying the Bible, but if we don't translate it into action, we have totally missed the point. In James 1:22, we're told that we shouldn't just hear the Word of God; we are to "do what it says." So what qualities should be found in a good resolution? It should be **personal** (use *I, me, my, mine*), it should be **possible** (don't choose something so far-fetched that you'll just become discouraged), it should be **measurable** (a specific goal to achieve within a specific time period), and it should be **action oriented** (not just a spiritual thought).

Examples:

1. I sometimes struggle to really believe that God loves me unconditionally. My head gets full of lies about my worth. In order to focus on the truth, I will write down one of the verses from Day One about God's love for me. I'll post it in places that I see regularly—on the dashboard of my car, on my mirror, by my bed—and will saturate my mind with His words about me.

2. I want to have a different perspective on God's discipline in my life. Instead of trying to run from it, I will recognize that it is one of the primary ways my heavenly Father is restoring me to wholeness. I will go to confession this week, and instead of viewing the sacrament as a punishment, I'll see it as a way to draw close to God and ask for healing.

3. I am going to take some time to reflect on whom God is calling me to serve. I will commit to *staying* and *being faithful* in that place, instead of looking for something bigger and better. I will daily ask God to help me to thrive right where I am, and for Him to make it clear when I should walk through the door of a new opportunity.

My resolution:

## Catechism Clips

**CCC 2851** In this petition, evil is not an abstraction, but refers to a person, Satan, the Evil One, the angel who opposes God. The devil (*dia-bolos*) is the one who "throws himself across" God's plan and his work of salvation accomplished in Christ.

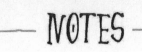

NOTES

# Lesson 2

# EMMANUEL ~ JESUS CHRIST

## Introduction

Who is Jesus Christ? It may seem strange to begin with such a seemingly simple question, but it's one that even Jesus asked His disciples: "Who do the crowds say that I am?" (Luke 9:18). The disciples answered by telling Him how people of the day were describing Him. Some were saying Jesus was "John the Baptist, others, Elijah; still others, 'one of the ancient prophets has arisen'" (Luke 9:19). In our current culture, some people describe Jesus as a great teacher, a moral leader, and someone who showed us how to love.

We know from the Bible that Jesus was fully human. He had a human body, which grew tired (John 4:6) and got hungry (Matthew 4:2). Jesus had human emotions; He expressed anger (Mark 11:15–17), love (Mark 10:21), and sadness (John 11:32–36). He can relate to us because of His human experiences such as temptation (Mark 1:13), learning (Luke 2:46–52), work (Mark 6:3), obedience (Luke 2:51), and suffering (the Passion).

Was He more than a man? Was He more than a great teacher and a moral leader? To avoid the mistake of worshipping a god of our own making—a god of our imagination—we need to look at how Jesus described Himself.

"I am the bread of life." (John 6:35)
"I am the light of the world." (John 8:12)
"I am the resurrection and the life." (John 11:25)
"I am the way, the truth, and the life." (John 14:6)
"Receive me; receive God." (Matthew 10:40)
"To have seen me is to have seen God." (John 14:9)

Author C. S. Lewis wrote:

A man who was merely a man and said the sort of things Jesus said wouldn't be a great moral teacher, he'd either be a lunatic—on a level with a man who says he's a poached egg—or else he'd be the devil of hell. You must make your choice. Either this man was and is the Son of God, or else a madman or something worse. . . . But don't let us come up with any patronizing nonsense about his being a great human teacher. He hasn't left that open to us. He didn't intend to.[4]

# Day One
# JESUS THE ANSWER

**Read John 14:1–10 and the following commentary on that passage.**

From ancient times philosophers have summed up the human condition as a quest to answer three fundamental queries: What should I do? What can I know? What can I hope for? Jesus Christ answers them all, not merely with doctrine, but with his very person. "I am the way" can translate into: What should you do? Follow me! Do what I have done. "I am the truth" means: What can you know? You can know everything, if only you know me. Knowing me, you know the truth; you know the secret behind the workings of the whole universe and the yearnings of the human heart. "I am the life" means: What can you hope for? In me, through me, you can hope for and expect the fullness of life that you long for, even though you may not be able to put that longing into words. Christ is truly the living water that quenches every thirst. He is truly the light that scatters every kind of darkness. The quest of every man and woman to satisfy the heart's deepest needs is the quest to seek his face, and it leads either to Christ and the place he has prepared for us in heaven or to a dead end.[5]

1. According to the commentary, what is Jesus telling us when He says, "I am the way, the truth, and the life"?

"I am the way" means:

"I am the truth" means:

---

[4] C. S. Lewis, *Mere Christianity*, rev. ed. (New York: Macmillan/Collier, 1952), 55.
[5] John Bartunek, *The Better Part: A Christ-Centered Resource for Personal Prayer* (Hamden, CT: Circle Press, 2007), 936.

"I am the life" means:

2. How would you explain Jesus Christ to someone who has never heard of Him? Describe Him in three or four sentences.

3. Using the letterhead stationery in Appendix 1, write a letter to Jesus. Correspond with Him as you would a friend. Share with Him your dreams and what you are hoping for, your fears and how you need His help. Tell Him what He means to you. Note: These letters are meant to be private. No one should be asked to share any portion of her letter in a group setting.

*Quiet your heart and enjoy His presence. . . . He holds the answers to the deepest longings of your heart.*

*At a time when Western women have more privilege and opportunity than ever before, our feelings of discontent and dissatisfaction have skyrocketed. Could it be that we are looking for answers to our longings in the wrong places? Could it be that we have become seekers of comfort instead of seekers of truth? Take some time to ask the Lord to help you to be open to Him when He shows you the way to go, instead of insisting on your own way. Ask Him to give you the humility to set down your preconceived notions of who He is and what is true, in order to hear and accept His perspective. Ask Him to replace your complacency or your willingness to settle for being comfortable instead of truly living the life you were created for. He is the way, the truth, and the life. Your heart's deepest longings will be satisfied only through a relationship with Him.*

# Day Two
# JESUS THE FULFILLMENT

*"[Jesus] said to them, 'These are my words that I spoke to you while I was still with you, that everything written about me in the law of Moses and in the prophets and psalms must be fulfilled.' Then he opened their minds to understand the scriptures." (Luke 24:44–45)*

The Old Testament is filled with several dozen major prophecies regarding "the anointed one" ("Messiah" in Hebrew), the deliverer who was to be sent by God at some point in the future to rescue His people. These prophecies were hints of what was to come, which would make it easier to identify whether a person was the true Messiah or an impostor.

Spoiler alert: Jesus nailed every single one of them. Some of us take that fact at face value, but others have a bit more of a skeptical streak. Didn't Jesus already know what was said in the Old Testament, so couldn't He just choose to fulfill each one? Actually, no. Many of the prophecies were tied to events (some historical, some personal) that a person just couldn't control.

Next objection: Wasn't the Bible just put together to make Jesus look good? Couldn't the New Testament writers just have worked the facts to make it all fit? For example, there was an Old Testament prophecy that said the Messiah's bones wouldn't be broken, so couldn't the writer of the Gospel of John have just *said* that the legs of the two thieves on either side of Jesus were broken, but that Jesus was already dead so the soldiers didn't break His? A number of things make it unlikely that one of the Gospel writers would have fabricated the facts. Why would they later have been willing to be martyred for the honor of someone who was a fake messiah? Why wouldn't the Jewish community (full of eyewitnesses) have jumped all over falsified facts? While the Jewish Talmud never refers to Jesus positively, it also doesn't refute that the fulfillment of the prophecies took place. On that subject, there is silence.

It's OK to hash out our doubts, questions, and objections. But let's ask the Lord to help us have the openness to really listen to His words—to *His* perspective on what took place. Let's seek truth wholeheartedly.

1. Read the following prophecies found in Isaiah 53 regarding the suffering Messiah, and note the New Testament fulfillments found in the verses that follow. Note: These prophecies were made more than five hundred years before Jesus' birth.

## Isaiah 53

1 Who would believe what we have heard? To whom has the arm of the LORD been revealed?

2 He grew up like a sapling before him, like a shoot from the parched earth; He had no majestic bearing to catch our eye, no beauty to draw us to him.

3 He was spurned and avoided by men, a man of suffering, knowing pain, Like one from whom you turn your face, spurned, and we held him in no esteem.

4 Yet it was our pain that he bore, our sufferings he endured. We thought of him as stricken, struck down by God and afflicted,

5 But he was pierced for our sins, crushed for our iniquity. He bore the punishment that makes us whole, by his wounds we were healed.

6 We had all gone astray like sheep, all following our own way; But the LORD laid upon him the guilt of us all.

7 Though harshly treated, he submitted and did not open his mouth; Like a lamb led to slaughter or a sheep silent before shearers, he did not open his mouth.

8 Seized and condemned, he was taken away. Who would have thought any more of his destiny? For he was cut off from the land of the living, struck for the sins of his people.

9 He was given a grave among the wicked, a burial place with evildoers, though he had done no wrong, nor was deceit found in his mouth.

10 But it was the LORD's will to crush him with pain. By making his life as a reparation offering, he shall see his offspring, shall lengthen his days, and the LORD's will shall be accomplished through him.

11 Because of his anguish he shall see the light; because of his knowledge he shall be content; My servant, the just one, shall justify the many, their iniquity he shall bear.

12 Therefore I will give him his portion among the many, and he shall divide the spoils with the mighty, Because he surrendered himself to death, was counted among the transgressors, Bore the sins of many, and interceded for the transgressors.

Luke 17:25 (fulfillment of Isaiah 53:3)

2 Corinthians 5:21 (fulfillment of Isaiah 53:4–5)

Mark 15:4–5, Luke 23:8–9, John 1:29 (fulfillment of Isaiah 53:7)

*"God has thus brought to fulfillment what he had announced beforehand through the mouth of all the prophets, that his Messiah would suffer." (Acts 3:18)*

2. Read the following Old Testament prophecies, and note how Jesus fulfills them in the Gospel of Matthew.

   "Therefore the Lord himself shall give you a sign. Behold a virgin shall conceive, and bear a son, and his name shall be called Emmanuel." (Isaiah 7:14)

   Matthew 1:22–23

   "But you, Bethlehem . . . least among the clans of Judah, From you shall come forth for me one who is to be ruler in Israel; whose origin is from old, from ancient times." (Micah 5:1, NAB)

   Matthew 2:1

   Other Old Testament prophecies include the massacre of the innocents in Bethlehem (Jeremiah 31:15, Matthew 2:18) and Jesus bringing light to Galilee (Isaiah 9:1–2, Matthew 4:12–16), being sent to heal the brokenhearted (Isaiah 61:1–2, Luke 4:1–19), being betrayed (Psalm 41:10, Luke 22:47–48), being falsely accused (Psalm 35:11, Mark 14:57–58), and being betrayed for thirty pieces of silver (Zechariah 11:12–14, Matthew 27:9–10).

*Quiet your heart and enjoy His presence. . . . The One who holds history in His hands is listening to you.*

*Was this prophetic fulfillment just some kind of an accident? Analysis by mathematician Peter W. Stoner concludes that the probability of someone fulfilling just eight of the prophecies is one chance in one hundred million billion.⁶ And Jesus fulfilled far, far more than eight! What do we do with numbers like that? We can't even wrap our heads around them. The response it should evoke in us is wonder and awe. At the very least, we should be pretty impressed with the fact that sending Jesus as the Messiah was God's intention from the get-go, and He didn't miss a detail in bringing it to pass exactly as He'd planned. Take a few minutes to praise God for being so far beyond anything we can wrap our heads around. Don't expect to figure Him out—just let Him know you find Him amazing.*

## Day Three
## JESUS THE SAVIOR

1. According to CCC 430, what is the meaning of the name Jesus?

2. Before we delve into why Jesus is the Savior, it's worth addressing the question, do we need saving? If we are basically good people, if our good deeds outweigh our bad, then aren't we doing just fine on our own? Explore this subject through the questions that follow.

   Can any of us claim to be without sin? See Romans 3:23 and 1 John 1:8.

   Why do you think we find it so easy to rationalize our mistakes?

   What is the consequence of sin—any sin, even a small one? See Romans 6:23.

The consequence of sin isn't the only thing that is a concern for us. Sin also has power—it can leave us feeling incapable of being the kind of people we long to be. We can get stuck—trapped—in patterns of behavior that we know are destructive.

---

⁶ Peter W. Stoner, *Science Speaks* (Chicago: Moody Press, 1969), 109.

Sin also divides. It puts up a wall between us and God. This is a very big deal, because we were created to have a relationship with Him. Close friendship with Him will be the only thing that brings us true satisfaction and fulfillment.

3. The punishment for sin is death, the power of sin leaves us trapped, and the division of sin keeps us from God. But God never intended to leave us in a hopeless situation like this. What solution does He offer? Is this offer made only to those who have cleaned themselves up and proven to be worthy? See Romans 5:6–8.

4. When Jesus died on the cross, "God was reconciling the world to himself in Christ, not counting [our] trespasses against [us]" (2 Corinthians 5:19). What motivated Him to do this? See John 3:16.

*Quiet your heart and enjoy His presence.* . . . *"If the Son makes you free, you will be free indeed"* *(John 8:36).*

*Without a savior, we wouldn't be able to experience freedom from the grip of sin. Meditate on the words of this beautiful song, "Lord, I Need You," by Matt Maher, from the album* All the People Said Amen. *Even better, listen to it and make these words your prayer.*

*Lord, I come, I confess*
*Bowing here, I find my rest*
*Without You, I fall apart*
*You're the One that guides my heart*

*Lord I need You, oh, I need You*
*Every hour I need You*
*My one defense, my righteousness*
*Oh God, how I need You*
*Where sin runs deep Your grace is more*
*Where grace is found is where You are*
*And where You are, Lord I am free*
*Holiness is Christ in me*

*Lord I need You, oh, I need You*
*Every hour I need You*
*My one defense, my righteousness*
*Oh God, how I need You*
*Teach my song to rise to You*
*When temptation comes my way*
*And when I cannot stand I'll fall on You*
*Jesus, You're my hope and stay*
*Lord, I need You, oh, I need You*
*Every hour I need You*
*My one defense, my righteousness*
*Oh God, how I need You*

## Day Four
## JESUS THE LORD

*"[Jesus] reflects the glory of God and bears the very stamp of his nature, upholding the universe by his word of power." (Hebrews 1:3, RSV)*

1. What did Saint Paul have to say about Jesus? Read his words from Colossians 1:15–20. After each section, put what you've read into your own words.

   "[Jesus] is the image of the invisible God." (Colossians 1:15)

   "For in [Jesus] were created all things in heaven and on earth, the visible and invisible, whether thrones or dominions or principalities or powers; all things were created through him and for him." (Colossians 1:16)

   "[Jesus] is before all things, and in him all things hold together." (Colossians 1:17)

"[Jesus] is the head of the body, the church. [Jesus] is the beginning, the firstborn from the dead, that in all things he himself might be preeminent." (Colossians 1:18)

"For in [Jesus] all the fullness [of God] was pleased to dwell." (Colossians 1:19)

2. What did the apostle John (eyewitness of Jesus' time on earth) have to say about Jesus? Read the following words from Saint John found in John 1. After each section, put what you've read into your own words.

"[Jesus] was in the beginning with God. All things came to be through him, and without him nothing came to be." (John 1:2–3)

"And the Word [Jesus] became flesh and made his dwelling among us, and we saw his glory, the glory as of the Father's only Son, full of grace and truth." (John 1:14)

"No one has ever seen God. The only Son, God, who is at the Father's side, has revealed him." (John 1:18)

3. According to CCC 84, what is the meaning of the title Lord? How did Jesus reveal His divine sovereignty or Lordship over all?

*Quiet your heart and enjoy His presence. . . . "[Jesus] is the Lord of the world and of history, the only One to whom we must completely submit our personal freedom" (CCC 84).*

*Submit your personal freedom. It's a pretty tall order, especially when we humans really like to be the ones in control. We'd be crazy to hand over our freedom to someone weak, someone we didn't trust, someone unreliable, someone selfish, someone driven by ego. But what would it feel like to submit our personal freedom to someone who had proven Himself to be utterly trustworthy, who promised to never leave us, who was completely selfless to the point of death, whose humility was incomparable, and who was the supreme power in the universe? What if we weren't meant to bear the weight and pressure of trying to stay in control all the time? What if there were a safe place to let down our guard? What if there were someone who was just waiting to guide us to the best place to experience joy and fulfillment?*

*Take a few moments to talk to God about what scares you when you think of submitting your personal freedom to Him. Then tell Him five things about Himself that remind you of His goodness and greatness, and write them down.*

## Day Five
## SAINT'S STORY

### Saint Victoria Wins the Victory of Love

Everyone wants a savior, but few people want a lord. Christ is both Savior and Lord. He is the one Savior: "Only in him is there salvation; for of all the names in the world given to men, this is the only one by which we can be saved" (Acts 4:12). And He is the one Lord: "And for this God raised him high, and gave him the name which is above all other names; so that all beings in the heavens, on earth and in the underworld, should bend the knee at the name of Jesus and that every tongue should acknowledge Jesus Christ as Lord, to the glory of God the Father" (Philippians 2:9–11). Jesus gave His life on the cross so that through Him we could experience the meaning for which we long, both here on earth and forever in heaven. He longs for our love, and when we get a glimpse of His beauty and a taste of the meaning His love can give to our life (". . . whose power, working in us, can do infinitely more than we can ask or imagine" [Ephesians 3:20]), we long to give it to Him. Saint Victoria had a particularly dramatic adventure of love once she decided to follow Christ.

Victoria lived in North Africa in a pagan family around the year 300, when severe legal persecution against Christians was frequent and violent. As a teenager, she converted to the Christian faith, though her family remained pagan. Soon she fell so in love with Christ that she desired to give her whole life up to Him, and made a vow of virginity.

Her parents were furious, because she was their only daughter and they had arranged a profitable and honorable marriage for her. They refused to accept her denials and forced her to go through with the marriage. But when the wedding day came, she put her trust completely in Jesus, and instead of going downstairs to be received by her husband, she said a prayer and then leaped out the upper-story window of her room. Landing safely, she fled to a nearby church and started serving Jesus and His kingdom full-time.

One Sunday morning a few years later, when she was in her early twenties, she was with a group of about fifty Christians attending a Mass being celebrated in a private home. Suddenly, a platoon of imperial soldiers burst in, broke up the Mass, and arrested the whole group.

Victoria and her companions (of every age and both sexes) stood trial, professing their faith courageously and eloquently in the face of torture. They were stretched on the rack, torn with iron hooks, and beaten with cudgels—just to make them renounce their faith in Christ and give due worship to the false pagan gods of the Roman Empire.

Victoria especially impressed both the public and the judges. Her brother (still a pagan) actually attended the trial and pleaded for her release on the grounds of insanity, but she debated so intelligently with the judge that she disproved the charge. The judge was so moved by her valor and poise that when his arguments and cajolery failed to shake her fidelity, he stepped down from his judgment seat, removed his robe of office, and pleaded with her, merely as a friend, not to throw her life away. She responded, "I have already told you. I am a Christian. And I attended the Mass."

Eventually, with all the Christians having firmly held their faith, the authorities lost patience and threw them into prison, where one by one, after long days of suffering that they bore with faith, hope, and love, they entered into the everlasting joy of their beloved Lord.

Saint Victoria knew who Christ was: the Lord who had given her both life and the hope for eternal life. And so He was the one Lord who deserved the gift of her life in return.

**Are there times in your life when you don't stand firm in your faith, when you downplay your Christianity to fit in? What have you learned from Saint Victoria's story to help you in those situations?**

Jesus always supplies the grace we need to do His will. If Saint Victoria's story disturbs you, remember that she was equipped with the grace and courage sufficient for the suffering she endured. God gives us the grace we need *when we need it*, not when we're worrying about something that might happen in the future.

## Conclusion

Have you ever tried to wrap your head around who God is, what He's really like? Jesus reveals God to us. Not that Jesus can be put into a box and neatly defined; He will always be more than our minds can comprehend. But would we want to worship someone so understandable and predictable that He'd just be a nicer version of us? Don't we long for something more—someone so much greater than we are that He can surmount the things that perplex us, bringing peace to our chaos?

May the many facets of Jesus fill us with wonder and awe whenever we think of Him.

May theologian John Piper's words increase our appreciation of who Jesus is:

> We admire Christ for his transcendence, but even more because the transcendence of His greatness is mixed with submission to God. We marvel at him because his uncompromising justice is tempered with mercy. His majesty is sweetened by meekness. In his equality *with* God he has a deep reverence *for* God. Though he is worthy of all good, he was patient to suffer evil. His sovereign dominion over the world was clothed with a spirit of obedience and submission. He baffled the proud scribes with his wisdom, but was simple enough to be loved by children. He could still the storm with a word, but would not strike the Samaritans with lightning or take himself down from the cross.[7]

Who is Jesus Christ? He is the lover of your soul. He is the eternal God, the Creator of the world, all-powerful and all-knowing, and He loves you personally. How did He prove His love? It was through His suffering and death on the cross that He proved once and for all your worth to Him. In the words of Father John Bartunek, "It's like sitting in the electric chair in place of the man who murdered your children so that he doesn't have to suffer and die—crazy love, incalculable love, unfathomable love. And that is God's glory: making known God's love."[8]

---

[7] John Piper, *Seeing and Savoring Jesus Christ* (Wheaton, IL: Crossway Books, 2001), 29–30.
[8] Bartunek, *The Better Part*, 932–33.

He is the answer to our deepest questions.

He is the fulfillment of all our longings.

He is the Savior who rescues us.

He is the Lord who can be trusted with our freedom.

There never was, and never will be, anyone like Jesus.

## My Resolution

**In what specific way will I apply what I have learned in this lesson?**

Examples:

1. During the prayer after the Eucharist this week, instead of mindlessly singing the Communion song, I will think about how Jesus showed His love for me by suffering in my place on the cross.

2. I'll take fifteen minutes this week to journal about the difference between Jesus being my Lord and being my Savior. I'll reread the first paragraph of the Saint's Story to aid my understanding. I'll identify one area of my life in which it is hard to let Jesus be in charge (being my Lord). I will pray that God will help me relinquish control of this area of my life.

3. Each morning, I'll reread the five things that remind me of God's goodness and greatness in the Quiet Your Heart section of Day Four.

My resolution:

# Catechism Clips

The following Catechism quotes are taken from the *Compendium of the Catechism of the Catholic Church*.[9]

### 81. What is the meaning of the name "Jesus"?

Given by the angel at the time of the Annunciation, the name "Jesus" means "God saves." The name expresses his identity and his mission "because he will save his people from their sins" (Matthew 1:21). Peter proclaimed that "there is no other name under heaven given to men by which we can be saved" (Acts 4:12).

### 82. Why is Jesus called "Christ"?

"Christ" in Greek, "Messiah" in Hebrew, means the "anointed one." Jesus is the Christ because he is consecrated by God and anointed by the Holy Spirit for his redeeming mission. He is the Messiah awaited by Israel, sent into the world by the Father. Jesus accepted the title of Messiah but he made the meaning of the term clear: "come down from heaven" (John 3:13), crucified and then risen, he is the Suffering Servant "who gives his life as a ransom for the many" (Matthew 20:28). From the name Christ comes our name of Christian.

### 84. What is the meaning of the title "Lord"?

In the Bible, this title regularly designates God as Sovereign. Jesus ascribed this title to himself and revealed his divine sovereignty by his power over nature, over demons, over sin, and over death, above all by his own Resurrection. The first Christian creeds proclaimed that the power, the honor, and the glory that are due to God the Father also belong to Jesus: God "has given him the name which is above every other name" (Philippians 2:9). He is the Lord of the world and of history, the only One to whom we must completely submit our personal freedom.

---

[9] The *Compendium of the Catechism of the Catholic Church* is a summarized version of the *Catechism of the Catholic Church*.

No program near you? No problem...it's easy to start your own group in your parish or at home and we will walk with you every step of the way. Find out more:

www.walkingwithpurpose.com/leadership

# Lesson 3

# NO LONGER SLAVES ~ FRIENDSHIP WITH JESUS

## Introduction

*"I no longer call you slaves, because a slave does not know what his master is doing. I have called you friends, because I have told you everything I have heard from my Father. It was not you who chose me, but I who chose you." (John 15:15–16)*

We all desire true friendship—relationships characterized by trust, affection, and support. A true friend wants what is best for the other. She is motivated by care and concern, not self-interest.

So why is Jesus Christ interested in your friendship? Is He lacking in some way? Does He need something from you? Does He want a relationship with you because He is lonely?

Jesus doesn't need anything. He was never lonely. So why did He create you and then desire closeness to you? The answer to this secret is shared in the *Catechism of the Catholic Church*, 221: "God has revealed his innermost secret: God himself is an eternal exchange of love, Father, Son, and Holy Spirit, and he has destined us to share in that exchange."

For all eternity, there has been an exchange of love going on between God the Father, Jesus, and the Holy Spirit. So why did He create people, especially when He knew how much it would cost—when He knew it would cost Jesus His life? In the words of author and speaker Christopher West, "Because love wants to share itself. True love wants to expand its communion. All the hunger we have for love, for union, for happiness are given by God to lead us to Him. The difference between a saint and the greatest sinner is where they go to satisfy that hunger."[10]

---

[10] Christopher West, *An Introduction to the Theology of the Body* (West Chester, PA: Ascension Press, 2008).

Jesus wants to satisfy your inner hunger and emptiness through a friendship with Him. He does this for many reasons, four of which we'll explore in this lesson:

1. He loves you
2. He wants you to fulfill your purpose in life
3. He knows you were made for more
4. He wants to spend eternity with you

Because Jesus knows you so well, He knows what you need. Because He loves you so much, He wants to give you what you need. What you need is *Him*. So He offers you His friendship.

*"Christ alone is the cornerstone on which it is possible solidly to build one's existence. Only Christ—known, contemplated and loved—is the faithful friend who never lets us down, who becomes our traveling companion, and whose words warm our hearts." —Saint John Paul II*

## Day One
# HE LOVES YOU

**Read Psalm 139:1–16 below:**

1 Lord, you have probed me, you know me: 2 you know when I sit and stand; you understand my thoughts from afar. 3 You sift through my travels and my rest; with all my ways you are familiar. 4 Even before a word is on my tongue, Lord, you know it all. 5 Behind and before you encircle me and rest your hand upon me. 6 Such knowledge is too wonderful for me, far too lofty for me to reach. 7 Where can I go from your spirit? From your presence, where can I flee? 8 If I ascend to the heavens, you are there; if I lie down in Sheol, there you are. 9 If I take the wings of dawn and dwell beyond the sea, 10 Even there your hand guides me, your right hand holds me fast. 11 If I say, "Surely darkness shall hide me, and night shall be my light"—12 Darkness is not dark for you, and night shines as the day. Darkness and light are but one. 13 You formed my inmost being; you knit me in my mother's womb. 14 I praise you, because I am wonderfully made; wonderful are your works! My very self you know. 15 My bones are not hidden from you, when I was being made in secret, fashioned in the depths of the earth. 16 Your eyes saw me unformed; in your book all are written down; my days were shaped, before one came to be.

1. Underline verses 13 to 16 as you reread them.

2. God created you with careful attention to every specific detail of your being. You are His masterpiece. He looks at you, His precious daughter, with delight and love. Does this truth agree or clash with your image of God's heart toward you?

3. Underline verses 7 to 12 as you reread them. Will God ever leave you alone? Where can you go to escape His loving presence? Is He with you now?

4. How is God's love for you described in CCC 220?

*Quiet your heart and enjoy His presence. . . . Rest in His steadfast love.*

*The Bible tells us that Jesus loves you so much that "the very hairs on your head are all numbered" (Luke 12:7). He knows everything about you—the good, the bad, the innermost secrets—and nothing diminishes that limitless love. While other people may evaluate you according to how you perform, what you achieve, or what you look like, Jesus cares for you simply because you belong to Him.*

*"God proves his love for us in that while we were still sinners Christ died for us" (Romans 5:8). He didn't wait until we were all cleaned up and deserving of His mercy. He proved His love when we were still a hot mess. And while this love is broad enough to reach every person, it is also intensely personal. In the words of Saint Augustine, "God loves each of us as if there were only one of us."*

*Take a few moments to thank God for His relentless love. If you find His love for you hard to fathom, ask Him for the grace to see yourself through His eyes of mercy.*

## Day Two
# HE WANTS YOU TO FULFILL YOUR PURPOSE IN LIFE

*"[For my determined purpose is] that I may know Him [that I may progressively become more deeply and intimately acquainted with Him, perceiving and recognizing and understanding the wonders of His Person more strongly and more clearly]." (Philippians 3:10, AMP)*

*"Why did God make you?* God made me to know Him, to love Him, and to serve Him in this world, and to be happy with Him for ever in heaven." (Baltimore Catechism No. 1)

1.  We are invited to know Jesus personally, which is not the same as knowing *about* Him or knowing *of* Him. Write down the name of someone you know *of.* Then write the name of someone you know personally. What aspects of your relationship with the person you know personally have allowed that friendship to grow deeper?

2.  Our friendship with Jesus grows deeper in much the same way that any earthly relationship develops. It doesn't happen automatically—we have to invest time and heart. Read the following verses and share insights into ways that we can get to know Jesus better.

    Jeremiah 29:13

    Proverbs 3:5–6

    John 14:23

3. Even when we realize that our true purpose in life is to know God, things can get in the way of that pursuit. Distractions, other loves, apathy, pride, and busyness are some of the obstacles we face. What do you find to be the biggest hindrance to growing closer to God through knowing Him better?

*Quiet your heart and enjoy His presence. . . . There's nothing more important than sitting at His feet.*

*Every single circumstance we face is an opportunity to know Jesus in a fresh, new way. Hidden within every heartache and every joy is a revelation of Him. Are you hungry to know God better? Do you want to fulfill the purpose He created you for? Then go at life with this perspective. As you reflect on the obstacles you are facing today, ask the Lord, "What are you trying to teach me here? What aspect of who you are is being revealed to me right now?" Then listen for His gentle guidance.*

# Day Three
# HE KNOWS YOU WERE MADE FOR MORE

Jesus knows that you were made for more than self-centered living. Because He created you, He knows what will ultimately satisfy and fulfill you. That *more* you are longing for is Jesus. So He offers you His friendship.

But let's be real here—it's hard to understand how to have a friendship with someone you can't see or touch. Without meaning to, you may end up developing a relationship with "imaginary friend Jesus."

In the words of Father Dwight Longenecker, the "Jesus" you are having a relationship with may simply be "a projection of [your] own desires, [your] own culture or values, goals and dreams of [your] own context . . . The real Jesus is bigger and more dangerous than your pleasant emotional experiences."[11]

---

[11] Dwight Longenecker, "A Personal Relationship with Jesus," Patheos.com, http://www.patheos.com/blogs/standingonmyhead/a-personal-relationship-with-jesus.

The only way we are going to experience the *more* we were created for is if we forge a relationship with the real Jesus. The following verses will point us in the right direction to do just that.

1.  A. What will we do if we are truly Jesus' friends? See John 15:14.

    B. How would you summarize Jesus' commands? See Matthew 22:37–38.

2.  Scripture makes it clear that Jesus isn't content with "Christmas card friends." He wants the real thing. Friendship with Jesus requires following hard after Him. How is this described in Luke 9:23?

When you are friends with Jesus, He shows up in every area of your life. And here's the hard truth: He doesn't really care whether or not everyone agrees with you, whether you feel comfortable, or whether you get every little thing your heart desires. He does care about where you spend your money, the words that come out of your mouth, and the attitudes in your heart. But more than anything, He is utterly consumed with love for you, and it's the real kind of love that truly wants you to *thrive.* That's why He gets into all those details of your life. He'd rather see you uncomfortable and passion filled than bored and purposeless.

3.  When we hold an area of our life back from Jesus, when we say, "This is off-limits and stays under *my* control," we are very likely to miss out on something really beautiful that He has planned for us. Can you identify an area of your life that you are holding back from Jesus, that just might be holding you back from living the *more* you were created for?

*Quiet your heart and enjoy His presence. . . . He longs to give you more than you can imagine.*

*In the classic book* The Lion, the Witch and the Wardrobe, *Lucy is preparing to meet the lion, Aslan, who represents Jesus in the story. She's frightened at the thought, and asks Mr. Beaver if Aslan is safe. He replies: "Who said anything about being safe? 'Course he isn't safe. But he's good. He's the King, I tell you."*

*The same could be said of Jesus. He isn't safe. But He's good. The life He leads us to isn't predictable, easy, or comfortable. But it is fulfilling, peace filled, and purposeful. The key word is* full. *Being a friend of the real Jesus, following Him wherever He leads, always fills the emptiness that so many of us feel inside.*

*Are you tired of feeling empty? Are you longing for purpose? Do you need something (or someone) to pull together the mess in your life and create something full of meaning? Then ask Jesus to give you more of Himself. This is a prayer He just waits to answer with a resounding yes.*

## Day Four
# HE WANTS TO SPEND ETERNITY WITH YOU

Have you ever asked yourself, "Is this all there is?" Have you pursued the things you've been told matter most (a good degree, position, reputation, résumé, home, clothes, body, etc.) only to find that achieving them doesn't satisfy as much as you expected? These things weren't meant to satisfy us, because God knows that when we die, each and every one of them will disintegrate into nothingness. Make no mistake—just because you receive the world's applause doesn't mean you've made the right choices.

This is one of the things Jesus wants to teach us through a friendship with Him. He wants to lead us to the choices that ultimately satisfy and matter in eternity. The most important choice you will ever make is one for or against a relationship with Jesus. Nothing will impact your eternity more than this choice.

1. How is heaven described in John 14:2–3?

*"Christ's words reveal that our destiny involves both a place and a person. The place is the Father's house, a place which will contribute to happiness; but being there comes from knowing a person— Christ Himself."* —Keith Krell

2. According to John 3:16 and 5:24–29 (spoken by Jesus), how can we receive eternal life? What is the alternative?

Ralph Martin, president of Renewal Ministries, addresses this important decision with the following words:

> Christianity is not a game. It's not a literary theme designed to enrich us. It's not a philosophical puzzle for the intellectually inclined to ponder. It's a cry of love and warning from the God who made us, who sees the desperate predicament we're in because of our own sins, who has gone to incredible lengths to rescue us from that predicament, and who is urgently concerned that we not overlook the only means by which we can be saved. Why be a Christian? Because Christianity is the truth. Because without that truth, life makes no sense and has no meaning. Because becoming a Christian makes an eternal life-and-death difference to each of us.[12]

3. Jesus offers us eternal life as a gift, but it's up to us to receive it. Read Appendix 2, "Conversion of Heart." Have you experienced conversion of heart? Journal your thoughts below.

*Quiet your heart and enjoy His presence. . . . There's no better time to surrender to the One who loves you and waits for you.*

*"The Lord does not delay his promise, as some regard delay, but he is patient with you, not wishing that any should perish but that all should come to repentance." (2 Peter 3:9)*

---

12 Ralph Martin, "Why Be a Christian?" ChristLife, http://christlife.com/resources/articles/whybeachrtn.html.

*God is patient. He waits for us to accept His gift of eternal life. But He doesn't wait forever. Death comes to all of us at some point, and its timing is unpredictable. Jesus longs to spend eternity with you, and it's going to be so incredible there! It'll be worth any sacrifice made here.*

*". . . no eye has seen, nor ear heard, nor the heart of man conceived, what God has prepared for those who love him" (1 Corinthians 2:9). Will you offer Him your heart?*

*If you aren't ready to do that, perhaps you could start to pray every day, "Jesus, if you are real, please come and get me." He understands that you feel lost. He knows that finding Him in the midst of the confusion in your heart feels impossible. So invite Him to come. Ask Him to find you. This is a prayer He loves to answer, but you have to ask. No one can do it for you.*

# Day Five
# SAINT'S STORY

## Kateri Tekakwitha

Why is Jesus interested in raising lilies from thorns? And why does He care about the hidden stories of little souls?

It is because each of us is the Father's gift to the Son. Each of us is an unrepeatable, unique marvel of God's creation, forged in darkness. No matter how humble or undesirable our circumstances are by the world's standards, God loves us with an unquenchable, everlasting love.

Kateri Tekakwitha's story is a humble one, yet she experienced closeness to God and was honored by the Church by being canonized a saint. She was born in 1656 to a Mohawk chief and a Catholic Algonquin mother, but a smallpox epidemic left her orphaned, permanently scarred, and partially blind at the age of four. She was a hidden soul in many ways, often shielding herself under blankets from the mean stares of other villagers and from the harsh light of the sun.

She spent much time alone, working in the fields and tending to crops, or in the woods collecting firewood and roots for dyes and medicines. During this time she would lift her heart to God, listening for Him to speak through the rustling of the leaves. She experienced God's presence, and always found Him ready to talk with her and to comfort her in her distress.

She was baptized at the age of twenty, and incurred the wrath of the village for her faith. She refused to work on Sundays and was in turn refused food. Children threw stones, and she was threatened with torture if she did not renounce her faith. She endured this suffering nobly, offering her love for Christ, thinking of all that He had suffered to win her soul for heaven. Kateri Tekakwitha knew from a young age that Jesus Christ, Son of the Blessed Virgin Mary, was watching over her with a bridegroom's interest.

Eventually, she fled on a two-month journey two hundred miles away to the mission of Saint Francis Xavier in the Christian colony of Indians in Canada. There, she received her first Holy Communion, on Christmas Day 1677, and devoted her life to prayer, penance, and care for the weak. She did these tasks as acts of love to the One who loved her first. Living a life of pure love for Jesus is how she became known as the Lily of the Mohawks.

We wonder sometimes why Jesus is interested in our friendship, and why He cares for us in our littleness. We are not the great ones of the earth. We do not start wars or conquer nations. We do not command the multitudes. We are small. Our daily chores and fallen nature are struggle enough. And yet, we still dare to dream. We dream of a great and endless love; we dream of One who is always listening, who bends with infinite tenderness over our misery and washes away the ugliness we find in ourselves.

If you wonder why Jesus desires your friendship, ask Him. Ask Him in prayer before the Blessed Sacrament, where He lays down His life for you every day, hidden in the silence and darkness of the tabernacle. Ask Him. And listen. And do it every day.

Kateri Tekakwitha lived a short life, dying at the age of twenty-four. But in that time she learned that Jesus desires not just our friendship, but our love. He wants to take care of us and claim us for Himself. Each flower, no matter how small, has a secret center that belongs to God alone. It is already His, and it always will be His. If we surrender and open up to Him, we will come to understand what He told us about the lilies of the field: "Not even Solomon in all his splendor was robed like one of these" (Matthew 6:29).

**What did Saint Kateri Tekakwitha do to discover Jesus' desire for her friendship? What can you learn from her life to experience a similar discovery?**

# Conclusion

"Why would the Creator of the universe be interested in friendship with me? I'm not a person with power and great influence. Why does He care about me?"

To understand why God pursues friendship with you, it's necessary to recognize what He sees when He looks at you. He doesn't see someone of insignificance. He sees the masterpiece that He created. He sees His precious daughter.

What an incredible honor it is that the One who holds the world in His hands, who knows all and controls all, cares about every detail of your life. Not only does He know you completely; He wants to be known by you. He wants an intimate friendship. He has proven what a trustworthy friend He is. He gave up everything for you.

" . . . though he was in the form of God, he did not regard equality with God something to be grasped. Rather, he emptied himself, taking the form of a slave, coming in human likeness; and found human in appearance, he humbled himself, becoming obedient to death, even death on a cross." (Philippians 2:6–8)

Jesus became one of us in order to be the bridge to connect us to God. Other religions are characterized by man reaching up to God. Only in Christianity does God reach down to man.

If we could only see ourselves through the eyes of God, never losing sight of His unconditional love for us, how amazing our lives would be! We would do everything with the right motive: out of gratitude for all He has given us. We wouldn't spend so much time trying to please all the different people in our lives, living for their approval. We wouldn't constantly search for fulfillment through shopping, food, or pleasure. Jesus would be enough.

This is my prayer for you (and me!): That you, "rooted and grounded in love, may have strength to comprehend with all the holy ones what is the breadth and length and height and depth, and to know the love of Christ that surpasses knowledge, so that you may be filled with all the fullness of God" (Ephesians 3:17–19).

# My Resolution

**In what specific way will I apply what I have learned in this lesson?**

"'For I know the plans I have for you,' declares the Lord, 'plans to prosper you and not to harm you, plans to give you hope and a future.'" (Jeremiah 29:11)

Examples:

1. I'll tape an index card with the verse Jeremiah 29:11 on the dashboard of my car to remind me throughout the day of this important truth.

2. Each time I wash my hair, I'll remember that "the very hairs on [my] head are all numbered" by Him (Luke 12:7) and will dwell on God's personal love for me.

3. Knowing that Jesus desires my friendship and wants to spend time with me, I'll do my lesson each day, using it as a springboard to prayer, instead of rushing through the whole lesson in one sitting.

My resolution:

# Catechism Clips

**CCC 220** God's love is "everlasting": "For the mountains may depart and the hills be removed, but my steadfast love shall not depart from you." Through Jeremiah, God declares to his people, "I have loved you with an everlasting love; therefore I have continued my faithfulness to you."

**CCC 221** But St. John goes even further when he affirms that "God is love": God's very being is love. By sending his only Son and the Spirit of Love in the fullness of time, God has revealed his innermost secret: God himself is an eternal exchange of love, Father, Son, and Holy Spirit, and he has destined us to share in that exchange.

# Lesson 4

# SURGE OF THE HEART ~ PRAYER

## Introduction

*"To pray is to talk to God about anything that is in your heart: the things that bring you joy and the things that bring you sorrow; the successes you experience and the failures you encounter; your strengths and talents; your faults and weaknesses; your hopes and dreams. In prayer you talk to God about everything."* —Matthew Kelly

When faced with a decision, do you like to run your thoughts by a friend to receive her input? Can you imagine how your relationship with a friend would diminish if you never spoke to her about what is really going on in your life? As women, we need to share our hearts with one another—our concerns, our joys, our hopes—if we want our friendships to deepen. In that same way, we need to spend quality time talking to God, or our relationship with Him will remain shallow and we'll miss out on the incredible guidance He offers.

I remember sitting in Sunday school as a little girl, holding a plastic telephone, along with each of the other children in my class. "Prayer is just picking up the telephone and giving Jesus a call," the teacher said. "He's your best friend, and He always wants to hear from you. I promise you'll never get a busy signal!" We would then all practice picking up the phone and giving Jesus a call.

Sometimes we think that prayer is something we have to be good at in order to do it, when actually, it's one of those things we learn by doing regularly. Although there is great value in reading about prayer, ultimately, we need to just "pick up the phone" and have a conversation with God. He doesn't need us to impress Him with big words and eloquent phrases. It isn't about how articulate we are. We can come messy and just be ourselves.

While it's the time we spend in prayer that transforms us, unfortunately all sorts of things make it hard for us to pray. In this lesson, we'll look at three of these difficulties and explore ways we can get past them to grow in our friendship with Christ.

## Day One
# DIFFICULTY NO. 1: "I AM TOO BUSY TO PRAY"

Do you ever feel you just can't find the time to pray? We're so busy, and although prayer sounds good in theory and we have a strong sense that we'd be better people if we did more of it, we get up and get moving and there doesn't seem to be any room in the day to slow down and talk to God.

That's the reason we often give for not praying. But I don't believe it's truly the underlying issue. I'm not saying that our schedules aren't busy. I just believe that we make time for whatever is important to us. If I'm honest, when I don't pray, it's usually because I simply don't feel like it. There's something else that I'd rather do. I think I'm going to feel more satisfied by doing something else.

If we want to be transformed into the women God created us to be, we need to explore what's holding us back from prayer. Let's be real and dig deep.

1.  What obstacles most often keep you from praying?

2.  What role do your feelings play in your prayer life? Are they important? Why or why not?

Our feelings will always encourage us to do what's comfortable. But true love isn't always comfortable. Authentic love often requires doing something *despite* our feelings. This is true of all human relationships, and it's true of our relationship with God.

3. According to CCC 572, why is prayer a "battle," and why is it worth fighting through the barriers to pray?

*Quiet your heart and enjoy His presence. . . . He is near to all who call on Him (Psalm 145:18).*

*We live in a culture that values productivity, results, and performance. Because prayer, just like love, can't be measured in that way, it's tempting to put it on the back burner. Sometimes it just feels more satisfying to check some things off the to-do list than to sit quietly in prayer.*

*Whether or not we feel like praying should not determine whether we pray. We shouldn't pray to get something from God; we should pray simply in order to be with Him. Our willingness (or unwillingness) to "waste" time with Him says a lot about how much we love Him.*

*Dear Lord,*

*I want to love you more, I truly do. But if I'm honest, spending time sitting with you is hard. I can't see you. I can't feel you. I ask you a question and I only hear silence. This holds my attention for about ten seconds. Help me to switch my thinking regarding prayer. Help me to see that even if I don't feel like I'm having a mind-blowing spiritual experience, you are just excited that I'm turning my face toward yours. This is a little hard for me to believe. Do you honestly love me so much that my attention means that much to you? If I believe what the Bible says, then I have to believe that yes, this is how much you love me. Help me to love you in return with the gift of my time.*

# Day Two
# DIFFICULTY NO. 2: "I WANT TO BE SELF-SUFFICIENT"

I hate to be weak and dependent. When a friend does me a favor, I want to pay her back quickly so that things aren't uneven. Feeling indebted makes me feel like I can't get my act together. The irony is that one of my top love languages[13] is "acts of

---

[13] *The 5 Love Languages* is a great book by Gary Chapman. In it, he outlines the five primary ways we express our love: physical touch, acts of service, quality time, words of affirmation, and gifts. The premise of the book is that the way we express love is the way we want it expressed to us. We can love someone in our love language, but if the other person's love language is different, he or she won't feel the love being expressed as much as we'd like.

service." So the very thing that makes me feel loved makes me feel like I need to balance the scales. It's a little messed up.

This desire to be self-sufficient bleeds into my relationship with God. I want to come to Him cleaned up, like a member of His A-team, the one He can count on to bring home the win. Left unchecked, this strong tendency of mine really gets in the way of a fruitful prayer life and blocks me from experiencing His love. I'll never fully give God my heart (which is what He wants more than anything) if I don't know He loves me and is for me. So clearly, this prayer difficulty is an important one to work through.

1.  A. Why is self-sufficiency such a block to a vibrant prayer life? See Matthew 18:1–4.

    B. What are qualities found in children that you think please Jesus?

2.  What childlike quality of prayer is described in Luke 11:5–8 and 18:1–8?

Why did the friend who needed bread and the widow who needed justice receive what they asked for? Was it because of their strength? No. It was because of their weakness and desperation. They were so needy that they asked, and asked, and asked. They knew, beyond a doubt, that help could be given, that power was there, and they determined not to give up until they received what they hoped for. When we come to God in weakness and desperation, He can't but help us. He knows exactly what will help us, and He has the power to do it. Don't give up. Keep asking. Don't quit praying just before the miracle happens.

3.  When children ask for what they need, they ask *big*. They ask with boldness. God wants our prayers to be filled with the faith that believes the impossible can happen, because when we tame them we are saying that God isn't all that powerful, or that He doesn't really care about our dreams and our needs. This kind of attitude saddens His heart. He wants us to bring our most audacious hopes and

passions and our deepest hurts and disappointments and confidently ask for His power to pour out, for the miracle to come.

The alternative to praying big things is to reduce what we're dreaming of to something small enough that we think we can accomplish it on our own. This absolutely robs God of the chance to show us just how wonderful, powerful, creative, and amazing He is.

So what are your dreams? What are your big, audacious hopes? What are three things well beyond your reach that you wish would come true? List them here, and turn those hopes and dreams into a prayer. Ask God to do the impossible for you.

*Quiet your heart and enjoy His presence. . . . Your prayers are evidence of your confidence in God.*

*"Ask and it will be given to you; seek and you will find; knock and the door will be opened to you. For everyone who asks, receives; and the one who seeks, finds; and to the one who knocks, the door will be opened. Which one of you would hand his son a stone when he asks for a loaf of bread, or a snake when he asks for a fish? If you then, who are wicked, know how to give good gifts to your children, how much more will your heavenly Father give good things to those who ask him."* *(Matthew 7:7–11)*

*Our heavenly Father is the giver of all good things, and He delights to give. He encourages us to ask, seek, and knock, and He waits to shower us with just what we need. It's important to note that this passage does not say that no matter what we ask for, we will get it. He says He'll "give good things to those who ask him." He knows better than we do what we truly need, and what the best timing is for us to receive those good gifts.*

*Let's not miss out on any of the blessings God is ready and waiting to give us. "Let us confidently approach the throne of grace to receive mercy and to find grace for timely help" (Hebrews 4:16).*

*Take some time to ask God for what you need. Don't forfeit a blessing just because you never prayed about it or you gave up too soon.*

## Day Three
# DIFFICULTY NO. 3: "I'VE GIVEN UP HOPE"

It can be hard to hope. Have you ever prayed for something and believed with all your heart that God would come through for you? And then you waited. And all you heard was silence. And all you felt was discouragement. And the promise in John 14:14 ("Ask anything of me in my name, I will do it") started to feel like a cruel joke, a bait and switch.

When this has been our experience, many of us allow our hearts to grow a little bit cynical. We don't want to be naive. We're smarter than that. We can see the obstacles. We're very good at assessing our reality, and adjusting our expectations accordingly. We've decided that it's better not to get our hopes up, so our prayers become stale or nonexistent. Spiritually, we are just going through the motions.

In the words of Paul E. Miller, author of *A Praying Life*, "It's a short trip from determination to despair, when you realize that you aren't going to change the situation, no matter what you do. It hurts to hope in the face of continued failure, so you try to stop hurting by giving up on hope."[14]

If this is where you are, then you might have had a really hard time answering question 3 on Day Two. I understand what that feels like. I've been there. It's very hard to reopen a dream when you've spent a while lowering your expectations. Just as I said in Quiet Your Heart on Day Two, God doesn't promise to give us whatever we want whenever we want it. But I believe that when we have given up hope, it isn't just an issue of us learning to deal with disappointment. We run the risk of developing an inaccurate view of the heart of the Father. We start to think that He's holding out on us instead of lavishly loving us.

1. I realize that when we talk about unanswered prayers, we are treading on sacred ground. This is the place where hearts lie shattered, and tenderness is needed. But even as I say that, I think it's important to share an essential truth: At the core of our disappointment lies a lack of gratitude. True, God has not given what we specifically asked for. But what *has* He given? Read the following verses and what God has given in each.

   John 3:16

---

[14] Paul E. Miller, *A Praying Life: Connecting with God in a Distracting World* (Colorado Springs: NavPress, 2009), 182.

Ephesians 1:7

Ephesians 1:13

1 Peter 1:3–4

I could list pages of Scripture references that would reflect even more gifts from God, but I think you get the point. Please know that when I have you look up these passages, I am preaching these truths to myself, as well. All too often, I forget or take them for granted.

In a season of my life when I had given up hope, God led me to a Bible verse that pierced my heart. As I read Galatians 4:15, I felt He was speaking to me. It reads, "What has happened to all your joy?" It stopped me in my tracks, because I knew that my joy was *gone*. And I thought about people who had so much less than I, yet simply having salvation through Christ was enough to fill them with gratitude. And I knew something was wrong, and the one with the problem wasn't God.

2.  The best antidote to lack of hope is a cultivated spirit of gratitude. The key word is *cultivated*, because gratitude doesn't come naturally to most of us. We have to actively look for evidence of His grace at work in our lives. Take some time to write down the ways in which God has taken care of you and blessed you (in ways you might be taking for granted).

*Quiet your heart and enjoy His presence. . . . Cast your hopelessness at His feet.*

*Come to God in your need. Ask for His help to grow in gratitude. Allow His words to become your own. When you pray the words of Scripture, you are praying God's heart back to Him. Take the following personalized versions of these Bible verses and turn them into prayers.*

*Dear Lord, "Restore to me the joy of my salvation" (Psalm 51:12, RSV).*

*"May You, the God of hope, fill me with all joy and peace in believing, so that I may abound in hope by the power of the Holy Spirit." (Romans 15:13)*

*"May the eyes of my heart be enlightened, that I may know what is the hope that belongs to Your call, what are the riches of glory in Your inheritance among the holy ones, and what is the surpassing greatness of Your power for me who believes." (Ephesians 1:18–19)*

*Lord, "I do believe, help my unbelief." (Mark 9:24)*

## Day Four
# PRAY BOLDLY. SURRENDER COMPLETELY.

*"To me, prayer is a surge of the heart, it is a simple look turned toward heaven, it is a cry of recognition and of love, embracing both trial and joy." —Saint Thérèse of Lisieux*

1. After reading Matthew 19:26, what do you think Jesus would have to say about hesitant, doubt-filled, tame prayers?

When we pray boldly, it isn't because we see God as a genie in a bottle who exists to do our bidding or to ensure our personal comfort. We pray boldly because in doing so, we are acknowledging that there is absolutely nothing that God can't do. The question is not *can* He answer the prayer in this way, but *will He choose* to answer the prayer in this way. This brings us to the second point: Surrender completely.

2. In Mark 14:35–36, how did Jesus model praying boldly yet surrendering completely?

3. When we surrender to God's will in prayer, we are following Christ's example. What's another reason this is an important way to pray? See Isaiah 55:8.

*Quiet your heart and enjoy His presence. . . . Let your desires be shaped by Him.*

*"From the end of the earth will I cry unto thee, when my heart is overwhelmed; lead me to the rock that is higher than I." (Psalm 61:2)*

*There is a rock higher than you. His thoughts are not your thoughts, and His ways are not your ways. But He is not distant. He is very near, and utterly attentive to your cry. He hopes that you will pray big and bold prayers. He hopes that you will see His limitless power, and ask accordingly. But at the same time, He hopes you are able to humbly recognize that you don't have a mind equal to His. You are finite, and He knows better than you what is best.*

*Can you trust that your heavenly Father knows what is best for you? This is such an important question—so essential to our prayer life that it's included in the* Compendium of the Catechism of the Catholic Church, *575: "Filial trust is tested when we think we are not heard. We must therefore ask ourselves if we think God is truly a Father whose will we seek to fulfill, or simply a means to obtain what we want. If our prayer is united to that of Jesus, we know that He gives us much more than this or that gift. We receive the Holy Spirit who transforms our heart."*

*In Psalm 37:4, we read the promise: "Take delight in the Lord, and he will give you the desires of your heart." Something very interesting happens when we delight in the Lord when we pray. The very desires that God wants us to have are birthed in our souls. Slowly but truly, we become more like Jesus as we begin to want what He wants, when He wants it, how He wants it. We are changed. We are transformed.*

*Take some time to share your desires with the Lord. Dream wildly. Pray boldly. But never lose sight of the fact that your heavenly Father loves you, and will only give you good gifts. And only He knows which gifts are the best.*

# Day Five
# SAINT'S STORY

## Saint Elizabeth of Portugal Rules from Her Knees

Prayer is simply speaking with God or, as Saint Teresa of Ávila put it, having a conversation with the "one who I know loves me." We can pray in the midst of our other activities simply by lifting our hearts and minds to God, thanking Him for His blessings, and asking for His help. But since our relationship with Jesus really is a *relationship*, we also need to spend quality time exclusively with the Lord, reflecting on His Word, letting Him pour His grace gently into our minds and hearts, and contemplating His goodness. When Jesus told us, "Seek first the Kingdom of God and his righteousness, and all these other things will be given to you as well" (Matthew 6:33), that's what He meant. If we put God first (which is what prayer is all about), He will guide us in all things and make our lives into beautiful works of art. Saint Elizabeth of Portugal exemplified this truth in a remarkable way.

Elizabeth lived in the 1300s. She was the daughter of a Spanish king, and as a child, she lapped up the lessons of self-discipline, modesty, and elegance that were taught in her father's court. She learned to be a model Catholic princess, though she learned it through simple, ordinary means. She was taught to conscientiously care for her appearance, since she was the daughter of a king (and of the King), but never to flaunt her beauty, lest she become proud or lead men into sin. She learned self-control and self-discipline by abstaining from spontaneous snacks and following a detailed daily schedule. She learned love for God and for her neighbor by participating in works of charity and in the sacred liturgy from a very young age.

When she was twelve she was married to the King of Portugal (Denis was his name), who admired her beauty and nobility of birth much more than her virtue. Denis was a cruel and unfaithful husband, but Elizabeth loved him with Christian charity and served with undying devotion, hoping and praying constantly for his return to a life of grace, and bathing him in cheerful and sincere attention. She ran the royal household with such generosity and good sense that Denis was free to dedicate himself entirely to putting his realm in order, and he was an effective ruler. Elizabeth found time to give constant service to the poor, and even to defuse political powder kegs. Twice, in fact, she rode right out into the middle of battlefields to reconcile opposing forces. When Denis died after a long illness, through which Elizabeth nursed him unwearyingly, she longed to retire into a convent of Poor Clares that she had built, but she was convinced she was to remain engaged in court life, much to the benefit of her children and other relations—not to mention the people of her country.

When we hear about such extraordinary Christians as Saint Elizabeth of Portugal, sometimes we can think that they were just born that way. But Saint Elizabeth's secret was found somewhere else—in her simple but constant and sincere prayer life. She regularly rose early enough to begin her day with morning prayer and meditation, and went to daily Mass as often as she could, receiving Holy Communion regularly. And in the evening, in spite of her obligations and duties, both pleasant and unpleasant, as queen, she always made time to spend another ten or twenty minutes in her private oratory, speaking with the Lord about her family, her affairs, and His divine will for her life.

Prayer is not complicated, which is why children understand it so spontaneously. What's complicated is convincing ourselves that God really does deserve first place in our lives. As Saint John Chrysostom taught, "Nothing is equal to prayer; for what is impossible, it makes possible; what is difficult, easy. . . . For it is impossible, utterly impossible, for the man who prays eagerly and invokes God ceaselessly ever to sin" (CCC 2744).

**How can Saint Elizabeth's model of a simple, constant, and sincere prayer life help your own prayer life?**

## Conclusion

"Whoever remains in me and I in him will bear much fruit, because without me you can do nothing." (John 15:5)

There is such a difference between a faraway, impersonal God and the One who remains within our hearts offering us a personal relationship with Him.

I see the difference, but I don't always live it. I have spent far too many days worrying and anxious. I can expend a ton of time and energy being concerned about everything that I have to do, making lists and feeling exhausted merely anticipating what is to come. At other times, I simply lay it all out in front of God in prayer, asking that He will engineer events, making the crooked places straight and giving me the energy and help I need one day at a time. It's amazing how much easier everything becomes when I let my schedule "remain in Him."

I have found that I cannot remain in Him throughout the day unless that is how I have started it. The beginning of my day sets the tone for the rest of it. One of the first times I was exposed to the importance of starting my day with some time remaining in Christ was when I read a book called *Disciplines of the Beautiful Woman*. The author, Anne Ortlund, had a wonderfully organized desk, purse, closet, life . . . and her book told her readers how they could duplicate that organization in their lives. Anne showered each morning and then went to a coffee shop, where a person could see the real secret of her life: Not a day went by when she didn't begin with prayer and Bible reading, remaining in Christ. While I really wanted to be able to emulate her self-discipline, I remember thinking, "Well, wouldn't that be great if I had time to go to a coffee shop each morning! I've got too much to get done. Do I need to get up at four a.m. in order to remain in Christ?"

The answer is no. You don't have to go to a coffee shop daily, nor do you need to give up all your sleep. But you can watch for the first quiet opportunity. There have been times in my life when I could get up at six a.m. daily and have an hour alone with God. There have been seasons when I desperately needed my sleep. I would then look for the first spot of quiet and claim it for God—not for social media, my endless to-do list, or Netflix. I wasn't always able to set a specific time, but I learned to watch for a pocket of quiet, recognize it when it came along, and reserve it for God.

One of the most esteemed sons of the Church, Brother Lawrence, has a lot to teach us about finding time to pray when taking care of all that life demands of us. When he would go to the kitchen to begin his duties as a cook with the Carmelite monks, he would pray, "Oh, my God, since thou art with me, and I must now, in obedience to thy commands, apply my mind to these outward things, I beseech thee to grant me the grace to continue in thy presence; and to this end do thou prosper me with thy assistance."

Was Brother Lawrence praying only while attending Mass? No. He was communing with God in the midst of washing dishes. He went on to write, "And in the noise and clatter of my kitchen, while several persons are at the same time calling for different things, I possess God in as great tranquility as if I were upon my knees at the Blessed Sacrament."[15] Also, he asked God to give him "grace to continue" to remain in Christ. He didn't try to do it in his own strength; he understood the pointlessness of it, just as it says in John 15:4: "As the branch cannot bear fruit by itself, unless it abides in the vine, neither can you, unless you abide in me."

Do you find it hard to pray? Is it a struggle to find the time? Ask God to help you. He is always listening and calling to your heart.

---

[15] Brother Lawrence, *The Practice of the Presence of God* (Old Tappan, NJ: Revell, 1958), 9.

# My Resolution

**In what specific way will I apply what I have learned in this lesson?**

Examples:

1. I will set my alarm fifteen minutes earlier so that I can *get up* (praying in bed doesn't tend to go so well) and pray before distractions get in the way of my time with God.

2. This week I will look for an extra opportunity to pray, perhaps while I am in the car, taking a shower, or washing the dishes.

3. When I sit down to pray, I'll make sure my cell phone is somewhere else, because it's such a distraction.

My resolution:

# Catechism Clips

Note: Both Catechism Clips are from the *Compendium of the Catechism of the Catholic Church*.

### 572. Why is prayer a "battle"?
Prayer is a gift of grace, but it always presupposes a determined response on our part because those who pray "battle" against themselves, their surroundings, and especially the Tempter who does all he can to turn them away from prayer. The battle of prayer is inseparable from progress in the spiritual life. We pray as we live because we live as we pray. Prayer increases our trust in God.

### 575. How may we strengthen our filial trust?
Filial trust is tested when we think we are not heard. We must therefore ask ourselves if we think God is truly a Father whose will we seek to fulfill, or simply a means to obtain what we want. If our prayer is united to that of Jesus, we know that He gives us much more than this or that gift. We receive the Holy Spirit who transforms our heart.

# NOTES

# Lesson 5

# SWEET GUEST OF THE SOUL ~ THE HOLY SPIRIT

## Introduction

Are you distressed today?
Are you facing a major decision?
Do you need relief from your responsibilities?
Do you have a broken relationship?
Do you find yourself falling into the same patterns of sin again and again?

I remember well a period of my life when I was overwhelmed with loneliness. I had moved as a young bride to Germany, leaving behind family, friends, a language I understood, and all things familiar. My husband traveled Monday through Friday, and I sat at home, nauseated with morning sickness. It was during this time that I began to really get to know the third person of the Trinity, the Holy Spirit.

I had not learned to fully appreciate Him until He was my only companion throughout the day. I couldn't afford to talk to my mom on the phone whenever I felt like it. But I could pick up a phone spiritually and talk to God whenever I needed or wanted to. I didn't feel like I was accomplishing anything in terms of a career or moving forward in building my new life overseas, but I was able to devote many hours to studying Scripture and growing in that area of my life. I didn't have access to wonderful Bible teachers or exciting Sunday homilies, but the Holy Spirit was a wonderful teacher, and I learned how to study the Bible and hear God's voice while I sat alone in my home. When Jesus promised the disciples that He was going to send the Holy Spirit to them, He described the Spirit as "the paraclete." The translation of *paraclete* is "he who is called to one's side" and "consoler" (CCC 692). When I opened my heart to Christ, He in turn sent the One who was called to my side. He consoled me in my loneliness and never left me.

Perhaps God is working in your life right now in the midst of circumstances that really hurt. Could it be that you now have an opportunity to get to know the Holy

Spirit on a more personal level as you come face-to-face with your loneliness, your emptiness, or your brokenness, and your need of Him?

## Day One
# GOD'S PERSONAL BREATH

Before we delve into what we can learn about the Holy Spirit, it's important to understand that we will never completely figure Him out. He is God, the third person of the Trinity. He can't be put in a little box of a definition and tied with a bow of complete understanding. As it says in Deuteronomy 29:28, NAB, "The hidden things belong to the Lord our God." We have to accept that we'll never comprehend the hidden things. But the second part of the verse offers encouragement for us: "But the revealed things are for us and for our children forever." So we're going to study the revealed things that are ours. God has made these things known to us and wants us to know the Holy Spirit so He can help us grow closer to Him and be more like His Son.

1. Is the Holy Spirit equal to God the Father and Jesus? See CCC 685. Note: The word *consubstantial* means "of the same substance or essence."

2. Let's take a look at the Holy Spirit's first appearance in the Bible. What action took place in Genesis 1:2?

The phrase used in this passage, "a mighty wind," is a translation of the Hebrew word *ruah*. According to CCC 691, "The term 'Spirit' translates the Hebrew word *ruah*, which in its primary sense, means breath, air, wind. Jesus indeed uses the sensory image of the wind [to describe] him who is personally God's breath, the divine Spirit." This means that just before the world was created, the Holy Spirit was sweeping over the unformed earth, breathing over and stirring the waters. He was there at the very beginning and was fully involved in creation.

3. One could certainly describe God as a long-term planner. Even in the moment that Adam and Eve sinned, God was preparing to launch His rescue plan.[16] Exactly how the rescue would take place and who specifically would be the Savior (the Messiah) wasn't clear to the people of the Old Testament. This "hiddenness" is described in CCC 702: "From the beginning until 'the fullness of time,'[17] the joint mission of the Father's Word [Jesus] and [the Holy] Spirit remains *hidden*, but it is at work. God's Spirit prepares for the time of the Messiah."

As the Holy Spirit continued to work in "hidden" ways, the people of the Old Testament waited and watched for the promised rescue—for the arrival of the Messiah. The Holy Spirit was at work, filling particular people to empower them for specific things. Bezalel was filled with the Holy Spirit, giving him supernatural artistic and creative ability to make the temple beautiful (Exodus 31:1–5). Gideon "was clothed with the spirit of the LORD" (Judges 6:34) to give him the strength and leadership skills needed for victory in battle. The Holy Spirit filled the prophet Isaiah so he could speak God's words prophetically to His people (Isaiah 61:1–3). The Holy Spirit filled specific people for specific tasks, but His filling was not there for the asking. The average follower of God had no access to the Holy Spirit.

The Holy Spirit continued the hidden work of preparing God's people for their Messiah. A foundation had been laid and God had taught countless lessons about what it meant to be in His family. After that long period of preparation, something totally new was promised. Read the following Old Testament prophecies regarding what was to come for God's people. Describe the promise and record what you think they might have felt hearing these words:

"I will give you a new heart, and a new spirit I will put within you. I will remove the heart of stone from your flesh and give you a heart of flesh. I will put my spirit within you so that you walk in my statutes, observe my ordinances, and keep them." (Ezekiel 36:26–27)[18]

---

[16] See Genesis 3:15 for this first prophecy about God's rescue of His people. This is called the protoevangelium—the first Gospel.

[17] This is a description used for the time when Jesus came to earth in human form (the Incarnation).

[18] I realize Ezekiel is a very difficult book to find. I promise you, it is in there. (I bought Bible indexing tabs and it makes all this flipping around the Bible *much* easier.)

"It shall come to pass, I will pour out my spirit upon all flesh. Your sons and daughters will prophesy, your old men will dream dreams, your young men will see visions. Even upon your male and female servants, in those days, I will pour out my spirit." (Joel 3:1–2, NAB)

*Quiet your heart and enjoy His presence. . . . Let the breath of heaven surround you.*

*I wonder if you feel a little bit like the Old Testament followers of God felt. Do you look at the Holy Spirit as someone reserved for the special few, those somehow marked by God for a mission and a purpose that you think must not include you? Does He feel out of reach? If that's the case, listen to these words:*

*"Through his grace, the Holy Spirit is the first to awaken faith in us and to communicate to us the new life, which is to 'know the Father and the one whom he has sent, Jesus Christ.'" (CCC 684)*

*Do you know what this means? It means that if you are seeking God, if you feel faith beginning to awaken in your heart, you can be assured that the Spirit's breath is near. He is wooing you to come closer. He wants you. Can you take a little step nearer to Him by sharing with Him your needs? Ask Him to fill your emptiness with Himself.*

# Day Two
# THE HUMBLE UNVEILING

God had promised that He was going to pour His Holy Spirit into the hearts of His people, but the waiting continued. These prophecies remained unfulfilled for at least three hundred years. Why so long? We are told in Galatians 4:4, "when the fullness of time had come, God sent his Son." God alone knew the perfect time for Jesus' arrival. During that perfect time when God became man—when Emmanuel, *God with us*, arrived—the Holy Spirit became very active. This stirring of the Spirit indicated something big was coming.

1. Read the following verses and describe the Holy Spirit's activity.

   Luke 1:15 (This verse is describing John the Baptist, whose life's mission was to point the way to Jesus.)

   Luke 1:34–35

   Luke 3:21–22

2. Read CCC 687 below, and underline every phrase that refers to the Holy Spirit's actions and purpose. Then circle any phrase that reveals the Holy Spirit's humility.

   "No one comprehends the thoughts of God except the Spirit of God." Now God's Spirit, who reveals God, makes known to us Christ, his Word, his living Utterance, but the Spirit does not speak of himself. The Spirit who "has spoken through the prophets" makes us hear the Father's Word, but we do not hear the Spirit himself. We know him only in the movement by which he reveals the Word to us and disposes us to welcome him in faith. The Spirit of truth who "unveils" Christ to us "will not speak on his own." Such properly divine self-effacement explains why "the world cannot receive [him], because it neither sees him nor knows him," while those who believe in Christ know the Spirit because he dwells with them.

3. John the Baptist; Mary, the Blessed Mother; and Jesus all were filled with the Holy Spirit. Read the following verses and describe each one of them according to the passage.

   John the Baptist: John 3:30

   Mary, the Blessed Mother: Luke 1:47–48

Jesus: Philippians 2:6–8

Which character quality of the Holy Spirit do you see reflected in each one of them?

4. If you are looking for evidence of the Holy Spirit's presence, then look for humility. We can achieve great things (in both the secular and the spiritual realms), but the mark of the Holy Spirit isn't achievement or fame. When the Holy Spirit is the One at work, everything will point to Christ. *He* will be unveiled. *He* will be the One lifted up.

This sounds good in theory, but in reality, human nature resists this kind of self-effacement. Sure, it's easy to *say* that we want Christ to be center stage, but then we work behind the scenes to ensure that we are noticed a little bit, too.

Ann Voskamp, author of the *New York Times* best seller *One Thousand Gifts*, knows what it feels like to be noticed and suddenly listened to with great interest. But she points us all toward the path of humility with these words:

> No one is meant to stand really on platforms. Sure, everyone's got a platform under them—every artist, every businessperson, every person with a message, a service, a product, a community. And the movers and shakers would have us thinking that a platform is what elevates your visibility above the crowd so your message finds its audience. But there's a deeper current of Truth running through the cosmos: "He must increase, but I must decrease." A platform is whatever one finds under one's self—and the only thing that is meant to be under a Christian is an altar. The only call on a Christian is not to pick up a microphone, not to pick some stairs to some higher platform, but to pick up a cross . . . The only call on a Christian is to build every platform into the shape of an altar, to shape every platform into the form of sacrificial service.[19]

---

[19] Ann Voskamp, "Every Platform an Altar," The High Calling, http://www.thehighcalling.org/articles/daily-reflection/every-platform-altar.

And when we see sacrificial service pouring out of someone who doesn't ask to be noticed, we are seeing the Holy Spirit at work. Christ is being humbly unveiled in the life of His servant.

Humility doesn't come naturally to us. In which area of your life is this a struggle? Where are you wishing your contribution would be noticed or recognized? Where are you finding it hard to serve sacrificially?

*Quiet your heart and enjoy His presence. . . . He is meek and humble of heart (Matthew 11:29).*

*The Holy Spirit is meek and humble, and He will not force His way into your heart. Revelation 3:20 says that He "stand[s] at the door and knock[s]. If anyone hears [His] voice and opens the door, then [He] will enter." He waits to be invited in.*

*If we do invite Him in, one of the things the Holy Spirit does is search our hearts. One of the reasons He does this is to know how best to pray for us. So often we are blind to what is going on inside us. We're pretty quick to justify our actions, but the Holy Spirit searches us, and intercedes for us based on what we truly need. "And the one who searches hearts . . . intercedes for the holy ones according to God's will" (Romans 8:27).*

*Will you open the door and invite the Holy Spirit in? Will you ask Him to search your heart and bring to the surface things that you might not recognize within yourself? I promise you, as He reveals them, He'll do so gently. And then He'll be right there, giving you the strength and the courage to ask for forgiveness. And He'll provide all you need for transformation in the very areas of your greatest struggle. Invite Him in.*

# Day Three
# CLOTHED WITH POWER

While He walked on earth, Jesus showed by His example what it looked like to be filled with the Holy Spirit. Then, just before He ascended into heaven, He told His disciples, "I am sending the promise of my Father upon you; but stay in the city until you are clothed with power from on high" (Luke 24:49). They probably didn't need a whole lot of convincing to stay put. Jesus' arrest and crucifixion had shaken them to the core. When Jesus was arrested and people suggested Peter was one of His disciples, terrified Peter denied even knowing Jesus. After the Resurrection, Jesus found the disciples huddling and hiding in the upper room where they had celebrated the Last Supper. Jesus stayed with them for forty days afterward, and that certainly would have buoyed their emotions, but they were all too aware of how dangerous it was to be allied with Jesus. Staying in the city, waiting in the upper room and praying sounded like a pretty good plan.

But everything was about to change. Read the story in Acts 2:1–39. I know it's long. But it's juicy and worth reading every word.

1. What change was seen in Peter after he was filled with the Holy Spirit at Pentecost?

God had fulfilled His promise! The waiting was over. He poured His Holy Spirit straight into the hearts of His people.

The impact of the Holy Spirit in Peter made him a bold preacher, and also revealed a growth in humility. In Mark 14:31, Jesus told Peter that he was going to deny Him three times. Peter's reply revealed his self-confidence: "Even though I should have to die with you, I will not deny you!" We all know how that story turned out. In his speech at Pentecost, Peter stepped off the platform that highlighted his own abilities, and instead simply pointed to Christ.

2. When the people were cut to the heart by Peter's words, what did Peter tell them to do? What did he promise would happen if they did this? See Acts 2:37–38.

3. Whom was the promise of Acts 2:38 made for? See Acts 2:39.

Do you ever feel far off from God? Be encouraged! You are not excluded from this promise. It is for you! If you have been baptized, in that moment, the Holy Spirit took up residence in your soul. He wants to work within you to *be in you* all that you need. Your part is to clear the cobwebs between you and God by repenting of your sin. This clears the way for Him to fill you with Himself.

4. In what area of your life do you need boldness or power?

*Quiet your heart and enjoy His presence. . . . Repent and be filled with the Holy Spirit.*

*"Not by might, and not by power, but by my Spirit, says the Lord of hosts." (Zechariah 4:6)*

*Is there something you are facing that feels overwhelming? Does the mountain you need to climb look terribly steep, and does it appear impossible to reach its summit with all the burdens you are carrying on your back?*

*God urges you to keep going, to keep climbing. But He doesn't expect you to do it by relying on your own might and power. He wants you to rely on the power of the Holy Spirit. Lay your concerns at His feet. Spread out the obstacles before Him. Ask the Holy Spirit to search your heart for any way in which the obstacles are rooted in unconfessed sin. If He reveals something, confess it on the spot. Then ask that the power of the Holy Spirit would fill you.*

## Day Four
# WHAT DIFFERENCE DOES HE MAKE IN OUR LIVES?

After Pentecost, more and more followers of Christ were baptized and filled with the Holy Spirit. Some of them, inspired by the indwelling Holy Spirit, became the authors of the New Testament. Many of the books they wrote were actually letters written to the early Church communities to encourage and teach them. The beauty of Scripture is that it was written in such a way that it had relevance then, yet can speak to us today.

Each of the following verses shows us a way that the Holy Spirit helps us. Once we understand what the Holy Spirit does in a general sense, we can think about how that *impacts us personally*. So as you read these verses, write down how the Holy Spirit can affect your daily life.

The first is given as an example:

**Romans 8:14–16** (The Holy Spirit confirms that we are God's children.)

"For those who are led by the Spirit of God are children of God. For you did not receive a spirit of slavery to fall back into fear, but you received a spirit of adoption, through which we cry, 'Abba, Father!' The Spirit itself bears witness with our spirit that we are children of God."

*Answer: I sometimes question who I am and where I'm going. When I read this verse, I'm reminded that God sent the Holy Spirit to live in my heart to remind me from within that I am His—that I am His child, His beloved daughter. If I live my life from that identity, I'm so much more likely to make the right choices, instead of doing things to please other people.*

1.  **Galatians 5:22–23** (The Holy Spirit makes us holy.)

2.  **Romans 8:26** (The Holy Spirit helps us pray.)

3.  **Luke 12:12** (The Holy Spirit helps us speak.)

4.  **John 14:16–17** (The Holy Spirit remains with us.)

*Quiet your heart and enjoy His presence. . . . Let Him intersect your daily life and transform you.*

*The Holy Spirit is willing to do so much for us, but He is a gracious guest, and waits to be invited. He leaves it up to you. You can decide to just keep Him in the entryway of your heart, or you can invite Him to come all the way in. It all depends on how much power and transformation you really want to experience. Unfortunately, too many of us are afraid to throw open all the doors of our hearts to Him. We say that certain rooms are off-limits. When we do this, we miss out. The rooms we close off are often ones that contain pain that He is just waiting to heal. Or perhaps they are places where we're stuck in bad patterns of behavior, and He wants to set us free. Take some time to pray about the rooms that you are keeping closed off to the Holy Spirit. Can you open the door a crack and invite Him to enter? I promise you, the breath of His presence will be sweet and gentle.*

# Day Five
# SAINT'S STORY

## Saint Elizabeth Ann Bayley Seton

For those who suffer, the Holy Spirit is the invisible consoler, the friend who lifts us up again and again, giving us the strength to carry on even when we have lost everything.

It is easy for us to think of saints as a pretty picture on a holy card: serene face, radiant eyes, folded hands. But that is often not the whole story. For some, there were dark nights filled with tears, moments of confusion and anguish and uncertainty, sudden shocks of tragedy, gray days of tedium and dryness.

It is in those dark days that we most need the light and support of the Holy Spirit, our consoler, advocate, and guide. It is through Him that a deep yes is forged under the shadow of the cross.

Elizabeth Ann Bayley Seton's life was marked by suffering, even though she was a child of privilege, born in 1774 to a prominent Anglican family in New York. Despite her high-society upbringing, Elizabeth's childhood was quiet, and she spent much of her time reading, especially the Bible.

She became acquainted with suffering early on in life when her mother died and her stepmother rejected the children of her husband's first marriage. When Elizabeth's father traveled, her stepmother sent her and her sister to live with their uncle. Later, her stepmother divorced her father. The social stigma of divorce at this time caused a shadow to fall on their family, and Elizabeth plummeted into a dark period of depression.

She married William Seton when she was nineteen, and the couple had five children. When William's father passed away, he left his family to the care of his son, during a time when William's business was struggling to stay afloat. The Setons eventually went bankrupt, and to make matters worse, William began showing signs of tuberculosis.

In hopes of improving William's health, the Seton family traveled to Italy to visit their friends, the Filicchis. Upon the Setons' arrival, the Italian officials were nervous about William's sickness, so they quarantined the family in a cold stone lazaretto. A few months later, William died. A widow at age twenty-nine with five small children under the age of eight, Elizabeth lived out all the worst stresses and anxieties that come with being a single mother who has to provide for her family.

It was during this time that Elizabeth began attending Mass with the Filicchis, completely taken by the Catholic faith. There, working in secret and in silence, the Holy Spirit was leading her soul to the fullness of truth. Elizabeth eventually returned home to the United States and was confirmed in the Catholic Church in the early years of the nineteenth century.

Her American family was horrified to discover her Catholic conversion. More alone than ever, she continually went to prayer with a sense of utter desolation, reaching out for God because she had no one else to turn to. There, too, the Holy Spirit helped her find light, encouragement, and strength. He brought her to Jesus and gave her new life again and again.

Feeling called to start a Catholic school for children, Elizabeth found all her efforts met with failure, so strong was the anti-Catholic sentiment at the time. Finally, after many disappointments, she established a religious order, the Sisters of Charity, with the help of a bishop, and then founded a school for needy girls. From those humble beginnings in a small stone farmhouse came a great work of God: Catholic education in America was born.

God's will is difficult to understand, but the Holy Spirit can help us to say yes to it anyway. We don't have to understand everything that God does in our lives. We simply have to offer ourselves like Mary, the spouse of the Spirit, and say, "Let it be done unto me."

In a letter Elizabeth wrote to a friend on March 26, 1810, she gave the following encouragement: "Faith lifts the staggering soul on one side, hope supports it on the other, experience says it must be, and love says let it be."

And where is the Holy Spirit in this struggle to follow God? He is the wind beneath our wings.

**What fruits and gifts of the Holy Spirit did Saint Elizabeth Ann Bayley Seton's life reveal?**

# Conclusion

*"Now the Lord is the Spirit, and where the Spirit of the Lord is, there is freedom." (2 Corinthians 3:17)*

There are so many times in our lives when we whisper, "I can't."

*I can't be more patient.*
*I can't forgive him.*
*I can't keep going.*
*I can't bear this loss.*
*I can't give any more.*

The Holy Spirit comes to us in those moments and whispers:

I know you can't. I see. I see your limitations. I see your hurts. I see what's been done to you. But even though you can't, I can. I have come to break all the chains that keep you from living the life of freedom that you were meant to live. You were made for more, daughter of God. I am here for you. I am for you. My love for you is relentless.

I am your **Comforter** (one who relieves another of distress).
I am your **Counselor** (one whose profession it is to give advice and manage causes).
I am your **Helper** (one who furnishes another with relief or support).
I am your **Intercessor** (one who acts between parties to reconcile differences).
I am your **Strengthener** (one who causes you to grow, become stronger, endure, and resist attacks).

Is there a place in your life where you are not living in freedom?

Do you feel chained to old habits of behavior and powerless to change?

Do you feel bound by lies about your identity—lies that say you are worthless, or ugly, or stupid?

Do you feel stuck in the rat race, unable to slow down, unable to breathe?

These are the very places where you need to invite me to come and set you free.

Don't treat me as an interesting character in a book. Ask me to jump off the pages of the Bible and into your heart.

# My Resolution

**In what specific way will I apply what I have learned in this lesson?**

Examples:

1. This week I will start every day by reading Romans 8:14–16. I'll remind myself who I am. I am God's beloved daughter. The Holy Spirit in my heart confirms it.

2. This week I'll pray God's own words back to Him by turning this verse into a daily prayer:

   "Teach me to do your will, for you are my God. May your kind Spirit guide me on ground that is level." (Psalm 143:10)

3. I'll choose one of the fruits of the Holy Spirit listed in Galatians 5:22–23 and focus on growing in that area this week, through the help of the Holy Spirit.

My resolution:

# Catechism Clips

**CCC 691** "Holy Spirit" is the proper name of the one whom we adore and glorify with the Father and the Son. The Church has received this name from the Lord and professes it in the Baptism of her new children.

> The term "Spirit" translates the Hebrew word *ruah*, which in its primary sense, means breath, air, wind. Jesus indeed uses the sensory image of the wind to suggest to Nicodemus the transcendent newness of him who is personally God's breath, the divine Spirit. On the other hand, "Spirit" and "Holy" are divine attributes common to the three divine persons. By joining the two terms, Scripture, liturgy, and theological language designate the inexpressible person of the Holy Spirit, without any possible equivocation with other uses of the terms "spirit" and "holy."

**CCC 692** When he proclaims and promises the coming of the Holy Spirit, Jesus calls him the "Paraclete," literally, "he who is called to one's side," *ad-vocatus*. "Paraclete" is commonly translated by "consoler," and Jesus is the first consoler. The Lord also called the Holy Spirit "the Spirit of truth."

**CCC 685** To believe in the Holy Spirit is to profess that the Holy Spirit is one of the persons of the Holy Trinity, consubstantial with the Father and the Son: "with the Father and the Son he is worshipped and glorified." For this reason, the divine mystery of the Holy Spirit was already treated in the context of Trinitarian "theology." Here, however, we have to do with the Holy Spirit only in the divine "economy."

**CCC 687** "No one comprehends the thoughts of God except the Spirit of God." Now God's Spirit, who reveals God, makes known to us Christ, his Word, his living Utterance, but the Spirit does not speak of himself. The Spirit who "has spoken through the prophets" makes us hear the Father's Word, but we do not hear the Spirit himself. We know him only in the movement by which he reveals the Word to us and disposes us to welcome him in faith. The Spirit of truth who "unveils" Christ to us "will not speak on his own." Such properly divine self-effacement explains why "the world cannot receive [him], because it neither sees him nor knows him," while those who believe in Christ know the Spirit because he dwells with them.

**CCC 702** From the beginning until "the fullness of time," the joint mission of the Father's Word and Spirit remains hidden, but it is at work. God's Spirit prepares for the time of the Messiah. Neither is fully revealed but both are already promised, to be watched for and welcomed at their manifestation. So, for this reason, when the Church reads the Old Testament, she searches there for what the Spirit, "who has spoken through the prophets," wants to tell us about Christ.

> By "prophets" the faith of the Church here understands all whom the Holy Spirit inspired in living proclamation and the composition of the sacred books, both of the Old and the New Testaments. Jewish tradition distinguishes first the Law (the first five books or Pentateuch), then the Prophets (our historical and prophetic books) and finally the Writings (especially the wisdom literature, in particular the Psalms).

Walking with Purpose is a community of women growing in faith – together! This is where women are gathering. Join us!

www.walkingwithpurpose.com/find-program-near

# Lesson 6

# GRACE ~ THE DIFFERENCE MAKER

## Introduction

We use the word *grace* in many different ways. The prayer before dinner is called grace, a woman of elegance and poise has grace, a dignified man with polite manners has grace, and one can grace a party with his or her presence.

We can offer grace to others. A number of years ago, my husband and I received a phone call from our son's school saying that he had been caught cheating on a test and had been suspended as a result. My husband picked our son up at school and brought him to his office. One of the consequences he gave our son was spending the day writing the words "I will never cheat again" five hundred times. He wrote for hours, wisely not complaining. By five o'clock in the evening, it was clear that there weren't enough hours left in the day to finish the writing. My husband decided to give grace, not by saying that the writing didn't need to be done, but by sitting down and writing alongside our son. Together, they finished the five hundred sentences, and drove home.

So what does grace mean in the spiritual sense? The Catechism defines it as follows:

"Grace is favor, the free and undeserved help that God gives to respond to His call to become children of God, adoptive sons [and daughters], partakers of the divine nature and of eternal life." (CCC 1996)

The *Encarta World English Dictionary* defines grace as the infinite love, mercy, favor, and goodwill shown to humankind by God.

The grace my husband gave our son, which is the grace God gives to His children, is free and undeserved help. Both show love and mercy. But God's grace given to us far surpasses anything that we can show to one another. He doesn't just come alongside us, *sharing* the punishment that our sins deserve. He takes on Himself the *entire* punishment due us. After paying that price, He offers us the gift of being His children and spending eternity with Him. The Giver of All Good Things doesn't stop there. He cares about each one of us so personally that He offers us grace each and every day for all of our varied circumstances.

But before we dive in, I've got to warn you . . .

You have to gear up for this lesson. It plunges you into some theology that at first glance might make you want to yawn or cross your eyes. Stick with it. Don't be put off by vocab that may be new to you. Because hidden within these meaty passages is the stuff that we are longing for.

# Day One
# THE FIRST WORK OF GRACE

1. According to CCC 1989, what is the first work of the grace of the Holy Spirit? What moves man to turn toward God and away from sin?

Grace's first work is to draw your heart toward God. That first time you felt hungry to learn more about spiritual things? That was grace at work. That sense you get in your gut that what you are doing isn't really in your best interest, that God wants something different and better for you? That is grace at work.

God is always after your heart. But He never blasts through and forces Himself on you. He's gentle, and recognizes that conversion is a gradual process. He'll let you run after the things that you think will satisfy, and He'll wait. When you figure out that you want more, but view Him as an "add-on," as one thing among many that you hope will fill you up, He'll wait patiently. When you come to the point where you recognize He is the only One who can satisfy you, grace will rush in and you'll receive "grace upon grace" (John 1:16).

2. Grace does something else as well—it results in justification. List the descriptions of *justification* found in CCC 1989 and 1990.

In other words . . .

Justification throws our sins as far away from us as the east is from the west. (Psalm 103:12)

Justification renews the inner parts of us—the parts that are wounded and hurting and hidden. (2 Corinthians 4:16)

Justification makes us clean—as white as freshly fallen snow. (Isaiah 1:18)

Justification reconciles us with God. (2 Corinthians 5:19)

Justification gives us what we need to break free from the bondage of habits that destroy us. (Galatians 5:1)

Justification heals us. (1 Peter 2:24)

**And it's grace at work in our souls that results in justification.** Without grace, we wouldn't be able to experience any of these things.

3. According to Titus 3:4–7, how are we saved? Why did God pour out the Holy Spirit on us?

4. Grace's first work is drawing us to a point of conversion. The effect of conversion is justification. What do we need to do to experience all the benefits of justification? Think about your answer to question 3, and see CCC 1991.

*Quiet your heart and enjoy His presence. . . . He wants to give you "grace upon grace."*

*I don't know about you, but when I read about all the grace that God wants to pour over me through justification, I wonder why the heck I run after so much emptiness. Why do I think that distracting myself, or numbing myself, or losing five pounds is really going to fix the things that aren't working in my life? What I really want is healing. Freedom. A fresh start. And that's what God is offering me—using the word* grace *to describe it all. Let's reach out and grasp it with both hands.*

*Dear Lord,*

*I really want all the grace that you have for me. But I've got some things in my hands that I'm going to have to put down if I'm going to be able to receive it from you. Help me to lay down my self-*

*reliance. Help me to lay down my desire to keep everyone happy—my habit of people pleasing. Help me to lay down my determination to always be comfortable. Sometimes I have to get uncomfortable for a while in order to experience all you have for me. Help me to remember Saint Augustine's words: "God gives where he finds empty hands."*

## Day Two
# THE EXTRAVAGANCE OF GRACE

1. Is the grace of salvation something that we earn? See Romans 11:6 and Ephesians 2:8–9.

2. If we don't merit salvation (justification) because of our good works, does that mean grace is cheap? Does it come at no cost? See CCC 1992.

The grace of our salvation has come to us at an enormous cost: Christ's life. Jesus stepped in and took the punishment that was due each one of us. He didn't do this because our good works make us worth it. He deems us "worth it" simply because He loves us. He asks us to have confidence (faith) in *His* payment for our sins, instead of our own attempts to pay for them. "A person is justified by faith apart from works of the law" (Romans 3:28).

3. What is the source of our merits (our abilities, our achievements, our worth) before God? What role does grace play in this? See CCC 2011. Note: In this context, the word *charity* means "love."

When you think about it, there really is nothing for us to boast about. Even the good things that we do (our "merits") find their source in the love of Christ that He has put in our hearts. We stand before God because of what Christ has done on our behalf, not because of what we have done for ourselves. God pours out extravagant grace, and we are the fortunate recipients.

4. We can't deny that the grace God gives us is free and undeserved. So why do you think we find it so hard to offer grace to others?

*Quiet your heart and enjoy His presence. . . . The price has been paid. Rest in His grace.*

*We've grown up hearing that there's "no such thing as a free lunch." And so we set out to earn our place in the world. We eat our vegetables to earn dessert. We get good grades to earn good college placement. We get the internship to earn the job. We get the gym membership to earn the better body, which we hope will earn us the guy of our dreams. Everything worth having comes at a cost, and we are exhausted trying to get and keep it all.*

*God speaks into our weariness. He asks us to let go of the "try hard" life. He offers us His grace, and asks us to offer it to others in turn. Spend some time talking to God about what area of your life feels exhausting. Ask Him to help you let go of expectations—those others have for you and those you have for others. Ask Him to replace the expectations with gratitude for the grace He extravagantly pours over you.*

# Day Three
# THE RISK OF GRACE

*"But where sin increased, grace overflowed all the more." (Romans 5:20)*

When we read of the extravagance of grace, we recognize there's a risk. Won't people take advantage of this? Won't they be tempted to say, "Yes, I know this is wrong. But I'm going to do it anyway and ask for forgiveness later"? As Herod said in W. H.

Auden's poem *For the Time Being,* "Every crook will argue: 'I like committing crimes. God likes forgiving them. Really, the world is admirably arranged.'"[20]

Which brings us to the question, "Why be good?" This is exactly the question Saint Paul addresses in the New Testament book of Romans.

1. According to Romans 6:14, why is sin not to have power over us?

2. Read Romans 3:19–20. According to verse 19, why was the law given? What does verse 20 say we become conscious of through the law?

Let's unpack the phrase "under the law." This describes the way God's people lived before Christ's death and Resurrection. God had given them laws to live by. The purpose of these laws was to help them make choices that would keep them healthy, both spiritually and physically. But time and time again, God's people failed to follow the laws. They were unable to live up to those standards.

This is what Saint Paul was talking about in Romans 3:19 when he said that the law was given so that we'd all be silenced. We're silenced because we are aware of how much we fall short of God's standard of holiness. The alternative to being silenced is to justify ourselves by saying, "Look at how good I am! Can you see all the things I've done? I've earned your love, God!" The law acts as a mirror, and when we hold it up to ourselves, our voices fall silent as we see that we haven't been able to obey all that God has asked of us. Living under the law is hard, because we simply don't have what it takes to do it.

3. Romans 6:14 tells us that as Christians, we don't live under the law. We live under grace. Living under grace is living under a *new* law. According to CCC 1966, what is the new law?

---

[20] W. H. Auden, *For the Time Being: A Christmas Oratorio* (Princeton, NJ: Princeton University Press, 2013), 57.

This brings us back to the question, "Why be good?" The answer? *Because we can be.* Because everything is different now that the Holy Spirit dwells in us. What we cannot do for ourselves, the Holy Spirit will do *in us and for us*, if we ask Him. Please don't just speed past these words. Let the truth they contain sink in.

In the words of Father Jacques Philippe, "According to grace, we receive salvation and the love of God freely through Christ, quite apart from our merits, and freely respond to that love by the good works the Holy Spirit enables us to accomplish."[21] The law is not the foundation of our relationship with God; love is. It is love that motivates us to ask the Holy Spirit to help us live in the way that God desires.

4. What is an area of your life where you have been aware of falling short of what God desires to see in you? Have you been trying to "create your own goodness" instead of relying on the Holy Spirit to do the work in and through you? What do you think indicates a person is relying on him- or herself instead of on God to grow in holiness?

*Quiet your heart and enjoy His presence. . . . Let Him infuse your heart with the grace to obey.*

*"What then? Shall we sin because we are not under the law but under grace? Of course not!" (Romans 6:15)*

*Some people look at grace as the ticket that allows them to live however they want and just ask for forgiveness later. This kind of behavior can result when we look at God's instructions to us as ways He's trying to take away all our fun. But nothing could be further from the truth. Our heavenly Father wants us to be happy and satisfied. The commandments He gives us are there for our protection and to lead us to a place of health and wholeness. Why would we want to sin? It only leads to unhappiness.*

*Take some time to prayerfully think about an area in your life where you find it hard to do things "God's way." Ponder the fact that all He wants is what is best for you. Ask Him to help you to trust that obedience is what will truly make you happy.*

---

[21] Jacques Philippe, *Interior Freedom* (New York: Scepter Publishers, 2002), 114.

# Day Four
# THE SUFFICIENCY OF GRACE

1. Saint Paul wrote a letter to the church in Corinth, and in it, he talked about a thorn in his flesh that he begged God to get rid of. How did God answer his request? See 2 Corinthians 12:9.

The phrase "is made perfect" means "is given most fully and manifests itself fully."[22] Isn't that amazing? When we are at our weakest, God's power is most fully given and manifests itself most fully. That's a truth to cling to when we're at the end of our resources.

2. When we are in need of grace, we can immediately turn to God in prayer, and He will meet us in our place of weakness. Where else can we go to receive grace? See CCC 1966.

Even when we are struggling with a thorn in our side, God still asks us to love. He doesn't ask us to scrape the bottom of the barrel of our own resources and just do the best we can. He asks us to drink from His endless supply of grace, poured out on us through the sacraments.

Sometimes all we can do is lift up weary, empty hands and ask for the filling of His grace. I can remember a particularly difficult time of my life, when I could barely find the strength to pray. I knew I needed to persevere and remain faithful, but the most basic things seemed so very hard. My prayer became little more than the outstretching of my empty hands. My words were few, but the physical action meant a lot. It was my way of telling the Lord that I had nothing to offer, and I needed Him to fill me with His grace. I went to daily Mass, and found that simply putting my body in a place where I could receive grace had an enormous impact on my spirit. I believe the Eucharist gave me the strength that I lacked. Bit by bit, I was restored.

---

[22] 2 Corinthians 12:9 footnote, in New American Bible, Revised Edition (Washington, DC: Confraternity of Christian Doctrine, 2010), 274.

3. What "thorn" is in your side right now? I'd guess that you, like Saint Paul, would like God to just take that thorn away. Perhaps He will. Sometimes He does. But other times, He allows the thorn to stay, in order to accomplish His purposes in us. Why was Saint Paul able to deal with his thorn? See 2 Corinthians 12:10.

*Quiet your heart and enjoy His presence. . . . "Be strong in the grace that is in Christ Jesus" (2 Timothy 2:1).*

*"They that hope in the LORD will renew their strength, they will soar on eagles' wings; They will run and not grow weary, walk and not grow faint." (Isaiah 40:31)*

*Dear Lord,*

*This is where our hope lies. It lies in you. The renewal and strength that we long for doesn't come from the spa or from perfect circumstances. It shows up when we have nothing to offer, and fills up our empty hands. Thank you for the grace that strengthens and sustains us. Thank you for making it so that at any time and in any place, we can "confidently approach the throne of grace to receive mercy and to find grace for timely help" (Hebrews 4:16).*

# Day Five
# SAINT'S STORY

## Saint Josephine Bakhita

Sudan is a land well acquainted with suffering, having been bathed in the blood of genocide and ravaged by slave traders for many years. Josephine Bakhita was born in Olgossa, in the Darfur region of southern Sudan, in 1869. When she was eleven, she was kidnapped and sold into slavery. The trauma of being ripped from her family and sold and resold repeatedly was such that she forgot her own name; in its place, she was given the name Bakhita—ironically, meaning "fortunate."

Josephine Bakhita's life seems anything but fortunate. One of her masters' sons beat her so severely, she could not move from her straw bed for a month. Another master, an Ottoman Army officer, marked her as his property by scarring her body and tattooing her with more than sixty patterns on her breasts, belly, and arms. She was also forcibly converted to Islam.

Different masters took her all over Africa, and eventually to Venice, Italy. God was working through the circumstances of Josephine Bakhita's life, and it was here, through the Canossian Sisters in Venice, that she first heard the words of Jesus: "Come to Me, all you who labor and are heavily burdened, and I will give you rest. Take my yoke upon you and learn from Me, for I am gentle and humble of heart, and you will find rest for yourselves. For my yoke is easy and my burden is light" (Matthew 11:28–30). The heart recognizes the truth in such words of gentleness. By 1890, she was baptized and had taken the Italian Christian name Giuseppina Margarita (Josephine Margaret in English).

A few years later, when her owner wanted to return to Africa, Josephine Bakhita refused to go. The Canossian Sisters and the Patriarch of Venice interceded on her behalf, and guaranteed her the freedom of choice contained in Italian law. Legally in Italy, she was a free woman, the mistress of her own destiny. But in reality, she had become a free woman from the moment of her baptism in 1890. Even in her final years as a slave, she knew that the gift of baptismal grace had already set her free on the inside: "If the Son sets you free, you will be free indeed" (John 8:36). With Christ living inside her by grace, she knew that nothing except sin could ever enslave her again.

With her newfound legal freedom, Josephine Bakhita became a Canossian Sister. In 1893, she entered the convent, and in 1896, she made her profession. A young student once asked her, "What would you do, if you were to meet your captors?" Showing true grace and understanding, she answered, "If I were to meet those who kidnapped me, and even those who tortured me, I would kneel and kiss their hands. For, if these things had not happened, I would not have been a Christian and a religious today." With this spirit of gratitude and humility, she worked hard doing menial tasks in the convent, often saying, "Be good, love the Lord, and pray for those who do not know Him. What a great grace it is to know God!"

Josephine Bakhita would pray that you, too, would know this great grace and hold it in high esteem. Grace is the gentle Lordship of Jesus Christ. It is His life flowing through our veins, His heart beating inside ours. Grace is what sets us free from slavery and gives us our true dignity. It is what makes us daughters of the King. You are a daughter of the King, and your heart will always be free if you live in His grace.

**As you read and reflect on Saint Josephine Bakhita's story, consider how she was able to experience inner freedom despite the outward conditions of slavery**

that marked the early years of her life. Does this change your appreciation of Christ's grace?

## Conclusion

Have you ever felt a heaviness of heart, a sense of despair, or a deep-seated fear that your life will never get better? I remember a period of my life when discouragement and depression nearly blotted out my ability to feel God's grace.

My husband and I had been living internationally for a number of years. Something was making me physically ill; whether it was a parasite or emotional unrest, I never knew the cause. I spent a week each month in my bed, unable to keep any food in my system. I longed to go home; I was terribly homesick. When we were robbed by someone very close to us, the betrayal felt overwhelming. I felt unsafe, unsettled, and uncared for. Everything made me cry, and each morning when I woke, I longed to pull the covers over my head and escape back into sleep.

On one of my lowest days, I read this verse in Psalm 51:14, NAB: "Restore unto me the joy of my salvation." I realized that I had been given such amazing grace when God gave me salvation, but that I wanted *more*. Where was my gratitude? Why could I not appreciate all that He had given me in dying on the cross for my sins? How could I expect more from the person who gave His life for me? I knew God wanted me to experience joy because He had saved me. But how could I drum up feelings I didn't have? It seemed impossible. I was empty.

I sensed Jesus listening to the cries of my heart and saying, "With man this is impossible, but with God all things are possible" (Matthew 19:26). His grace was being offered to me: grace to help me to be grateful for what I had; grace to get up and just "do the next thing" even though I wanted to do nothing but cry and sleep; and grace to quit complaining about all I didn't like because it was only making me feel worse.

I knelt before God that day and said, "God, I know I should feel joy because of my salvation, but I don't. I just feel unhappy. Please, will you do the work of restoring that joy to me? I can't do it myself. I do promise this: I will quit complaining about all that I don't like in my life. I'll quit complaining to other people, but also to you. I'll stop asking you to bring me back home. But I only promise because I know that you don't forget anything. You know the desires of my heart. Even if I'm not reminding you, you know. I will try to trust that if you don't change my circumstances, you know what is best for me. But help me. I am so weak."

The progress was slow, but after about three months, I realized I was much better. I didn't cry so much; I could delight in little things; the peace of my heart was returning. And just when I thought, "It's OK. I can live here. I'm all right," my circumstances changed and I was able to move home.

I am so grateful that God led me through the valley of despair before giving me what I desired. What I learned along the way was such a gift. God's grace is enough. If relief had come sooner, I might never have discovered that game-changing truth.

Perhaps you are waiting for relief right now. If you are, I want to assure you that God *always* shows up. And not just at some remote time, far in the future. He is at work now—right in this very moment that feels hopeless, in this current set of circumstances that seems without end. While we wait our job is to remember. When has He come through for you in the past? Focus on this. Remember that our God is unchanging and He will rescue again.

Hold steady and rebuke the lie that says, "It's all up to me." The truth is, we have an all-powerful rescuer who never leaves our side. Reject the lie that says, "Things will never change." The darkest hour is the one before dawn. Wait faithfully. The light will come.

The very thing that we think will destroy us can be what strengthens and heals us. Suffering brings all sorts of long-buried things to the surface. Sometimes it's the only way God can get to those deep places in our hearts to set us free.

The psalmist wrote, "I would have lost heart, unless I had believed that I would see the goodness of the Lord in the land of the living" (Psalm 27:13). I pray you would not lose heart, and would remain steadfast as the storm rages. God is in the waiting. He is at work. You will see His goodness unfold, and the all-sufficiency of His grace.

"I know indeed how to live in humble circumstances; I know also how to live with abundance. In every circumstance and in all things I have learned the secret of being well fed and of going hungry, of living in abundance and of being in need. I have the strength for everything through him who empowers me." (Philippians 4:12–13)

# My Resolution

**In what specific way will I apply what I have learned in this lesson?**

Examples:

1.  I want to experience all the grace that God has for me. I'll grab hold of the opportunity for more of His grace by going to Mass one additional time this week.

2.  If I am feeling discouraged about an area in my life where I repeatedly make the same mistakes, I'll increase my prayer about that struggle. Instead of trying harder, I will pray more.

3.  I will write 2 Corinthians 12:9 on an index card and carry it with me to remind myself that in my weakness, God is strong.

My resolution:

# Catechism Clips

**CCC 1966** The New Law is *the grace of the Holy Spirit* given to the faithful through faith in Christ. It works through charity; it uses the Sermon on the Mount to teach us what must be done and makes use of the sacraments to give us the grace to do it.

**CCC 1989** The first work of the grace of the Holy Spirit is *conversion*, effecting justification in accordance with Jesus' proclamation at the beginning of the Gospel: "Repent, for the kingdom of heaven is at hand." Moved by grace, man turns toward God and away from sin, thus accepting forgiveness and righteousness from on high. "Justification is not only the remission of sins, but also the sanctification [growth in holiness] and renewal of the interior man."

**CCC 1990** Justification *detaches man from sin* which contradicts the love of God, and purifies his heart of sin. Justification follows upon God's merciful initiative of offering forgiveness. It reconciles man with God. It frees from the enslavement to sin, and it heals.

**CCC 1991** Justification is at the same time *the acceptance of God's righteousness* through faith in Jesus Christ. Righteousness (or "justice") here means the rectitude of divine love. With justification, faith, hope, and charity are poured into our hearts, and obedience to the divine will is granted us.

**CCC 1992** Justification has been merited for us by the Passion of Christ who offered himself on the cross as a living victim, holy and pleasing to God, and whose blood has become the instrument of atonement for the sins of all men. Justification is conferred in Baptism, the sacrament of faith. It conforms us to the righteousness of God, who makes us inwardly just by the power of his mercy. Its purpose is the glory of God and of Christ, and the gift of eternal life:

> But now the righteousness of God has been manifested apart from law, although the law and the prophets bear witness to it, the righteousness of God through faith in Jesus Christ for all who believe. For there is no distinction: since all have sinned and fall short of the glory of God, they are justified by his grace as a gift, through the redemption which is in Christ Jesus, whom God put forward as an expiation by his blood, to be received by faith. This was to show God's righteousness, because in his divine forbearance he had passed over former sins; it was to prove at the present time that he himself is righteous and that he justifies him who has faith in Jesus.

**CCC 2011** *The charity of Christ is the source in us of all our merits* before God. Grace, by uniting us to Christ in active love, ensures the supernatural quality of our acts and consequently their merit before God and before men. The saints have always had a lively awareness that their merits were pure grace.

> After earth's exile, I hope to go and enjoy you in the fatherland, but I do not want to lay up merits for heaven. I want to work for your *love alone* . . . In the evening of this life, I shall appear before you with empty hands, for I do not ask you to count my works. All our justice is blemished in your eyes. I wish, then, to be clothed in your own *justice* and to receive from your *love* the eternal possession of *yourself*. —Saint Thérèse of Lisieux

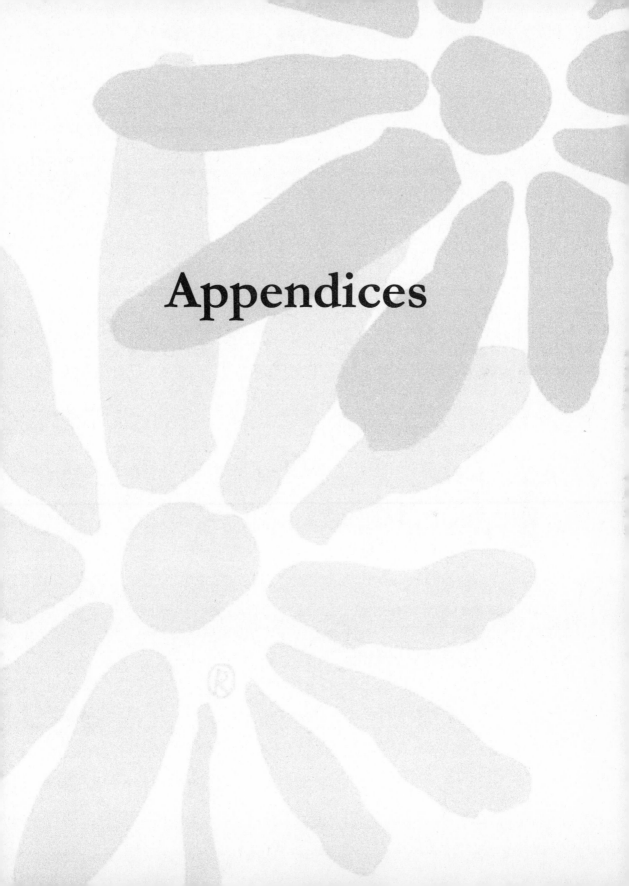

# Appendices

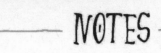

# NOTES

## Appendix 1
# WALKING WITH PURPOSE LETTERHEAD
# STATIONERY FOR YOUR LETTER TO JESUS

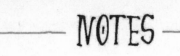

# Appendix 2
# CONVERSION OF HEART

The Catholic faith is full of beautiful traditions, rituals, and sacraments. As powerful as they are, it is possible for them to become mere habits in our lives, instead of experiences that draw us close to the heart of Christ. In the words of John Paul II, they can become acts of "hollow ritualism." We might receive our first Communion and the sacraments of confession and confirmation, yet never experience the interior conversion that opens the heart to a personal relationship with God.

Pope Benedict XVI has explained that the "door of faith" is opened at one's baptism, but we are called to open it again, walk through it, and rediscover and renew our relationship with Christ and His Church.[23]

So how do we do this? How do we walk through that door of faith so we can begin to experience the abundant life that God has planned for us?

## GETTING PERSONAL

The word *conversion* means "the act of turning." This means that conversion involves a turning away from one thing and a turning toward another. When you haven't experienced conversion of heart, you are turned *toward* your own desires. You are the one in charge, and you do what you feel is right and best at any given moment. You may choose to do things that are very good for other people, but the distinction is that *you are choosing*. You are deciding. You are the one in control.

Imagine driving a car. You are sitting in the driver's seat, and your hands are on the steering wheel. You've welcomed Jesus into the passenger's seat, and have listened to His comments. But whether or not you follow His directions is really up to you. You may follow them or you may not, depending on what seems right to you.

When you experience interior conversion, you decide to turn, to get out of the driver's seat, move into the passenger's seat, and invite God to be the driver. Instead of seeing Him as an advice giver or someone nice to have around for the holidays, you give Him control of every aspect of your life.

More than likely, you don't find this easy to do. This is because of the universal struggle with pride. We want to be the ones in charge. We don't like to be in

---

[23] Pope Benedict XVI, *Apostolic Letter: Porta Fidei*, for the Indiction of the Year of Faith, October 11, 2011.

desperate need. We like to be the captains of our ships, charting our own courses. As William Ernest Henley wrote, "I am the master of my fate: I am the captain of my soul."

Conversion of heart isn't possible without humility. The first step is to recognize your desperate need of a savior. Romans 6:23 states that the "wages of sin is death." When you hear this, you might be tempted to justify your behavior, or compare yourself with others. You might think to yourself, "I'm not a murderer. I'm not as bad as this or that person. If someone were to put my good deeds and bad deeds on a scale, my good ones would outweigh the bad. So surely I am good enough? Surely I don't deserve death!" When this is your line of thought, you are missing a very important truth: Just one sin is enough to separate you from a holy God. Just one sin is enough for you to deserve death. Even your best efforts to do good fall short of what God has required in order for you to spend eternity with Him. Isaiah 64:6 says, "All our righteous acts are like filthy rags." If you come to God thinking that you are going to be accepted by Him based on your "good conduct," He will point out that your righteousness is nothing compared to His infinite holiness.

Saint Thérèse of Lisieux understood this well, and wrote, "In the evening of my life I shall appear before You with empty hands, for I do not ask You to count my works. All our justices are stained in Your eyes. I want therefore to clothe myself in Your own justice and receive from Your love the eternal possession of Yourself."[24]

She recognized that her works, her best efforts, wouldn't be enough to earn salvation. Salvation cannot be earned. It's a free gift. Saint Thérèse accepted this gift, and said that if her justices or righteous deeds were stained, then she wanted to clothe herself in Christ's own justice. We see this described in 2 Corinthians 5:21: "God made him who had no sin to be sin for us, so that in him we might become the righteousness of God."

How did God make Him who had no sin to be sin for you? This was foretold by the prophet Isaiah: "But he was pierced for our transgressions, he was crushed for our iniquities; the punishment that brought us peace was upon him, and by his wounds we are healed" (Isaiah 53:5).

Jesus accomplished this on the cross. Every sin committed, past, present, and future, was placed on Him. Now, *all the merits of Jesus can be yours*. He wants to fill your empty hands with His own virtues.

---

[24] Saint Thérèse of Lisieux, "Act of Oblation to Merciful Love," June 9, 1895.

But first, you need to recognize, just as Saint Thérèse did, that you are little. You are weak. You fail. You need forgiveness. You need a savior.

When you come before God in prayer and acknowledge these truths, He looks at your heart. He sees your desire to trust Him, to please Him, to obey Him. He says to you, "My precious child, you don't have to pay for your sins. My Son, Jesus, has already done that for you. He suffered, so that you wouldn't have to. I want to experience a relationship of intimacy with you. I forgive you.[25] Jesus came to set you free.[26] When you open your heart to me, you become a new creation![27] The old you has gone. The new you is here. If you will stay close to me, and journey by my side, you will begin to experience a transformation that brings joy and freedom.[28] I've been waiting to pour my gifts into your soul. Beloved daughter of mine, remain confident in me. I am your loving Father. Crawl into my lap. Trust me. Love me. I will take care of everything."

This is conversion of heart. This act of faith lifts the veil from your eyes and launches you into the richest and most satisfying life. You don't have to be sitting in church to do this. Don't let a minute pass before opening your heart to God and inviting Him to come dwell within you. Let Him sit in the driver's seat. Give Him the keys to your heart. Your life will never be the same again.

---

[25] "If we acknowledge our sins, he is faithful and just and will forgive our sins and cleanse us from every wrongdoing." 1 John 1:9

[26] "So if the Son makes you free, you will be free indeed." John 8:36

[27] "So whoever is in Christ is a new creation: the old things have passed away; behold, new things have come." 2 Corinthians 5:18

[28] "I will sprinkle clean water over you to make you clean; from all your impurities and from all your idols I will cleanse you. I will give you a new heart, and a new spirit I will put within you. I will remove the heart of stone from your flesh and give you a heart of flesh." Ezekiel 36:25–26

 NOTES

# Answer Key

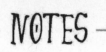

**Lesson 1, Day One**

1. God's thoughts are not our thoughts and His ways are not our ways. They are *greater* than ours, because His perspective is so much farther reaching than our own.

2. **Isaiah 43:4 (the first part of the verse)** I am precious and honored in God's sight. He loves me.

   **Psalm 139:13–4** He formed my inmost being and knit me together in my mother's womb. He sees me as fearfully and wonderfully made.

   **2 Corinthians 5:17** He sees me as a new creation in Christ. The old has gone away and the new has come.

   **Jeremiah 31:3** God has loved me with an everlasting love.

   **Psalm 118:6** God is on my side.

   **Zephaniah 3:17** "The LORD your God is in your midst, a mighty one who will save; he will rejoice over you with gladness; he will quiet you by his love; he will exult over you with loud singing."

3. **Psalm 103:12** As far as the east is from the west—that's how far God has removed our sin from us.

   **Isaiah 1:18** Our sins may be like scarlet or crimson, making us feel permanently stained. But God promises that if we ask for forgiveness, He will cause them to become as white as snow or wool.

   **1 John 1:9** If we confess our sin, God will forgive it, every single time.

4. Answers will vary.

**Lesson 1, Day Two**

1. God never slumbers or sleeps. He is your guardian. He's the shade at your right hand, making sure that you're not burned. Your relief finds its source in Him. He holds on to you so that your foot doesn't slip. He is guarding your soul at this very minute and forever.

2. **A.** We are wrestling not just with flesh and blood, but against spiritual forces. There's a spiritual battle raging around us.

   **B.** The enemy is referred to as a person, Satan, the Evil One, the angel who opposes God. When we pray, "Deliver us from evil," in the Our Father, we are not talking about evil as an abstraction. Satan is also known as the devil, and he "throws himself across" God's plan.

   **C.** No weapon that the enemy fashions to take us out will succeed. It will not take us down.

3. "We are afflicted in every way, but not constrained; perplexed, but not driven to despair; persecuted, but not abandoned; struck down, but not destroyed."

4. Answers will vary.

**Lesson 1, Day Three**

1. **A.** The Lord disciplines those He loves.

   **B.** We are to endure our trials as "discipline."

   **C.** God wants His discipline of us to lead us to share in His holiness.

2. Discipline brings the "peaceful fruit of righteousness" to those who are trained by it.

3. Answers will vary.

4. God revealed Himself as gracious and merciful, slow to anger and abounding in love and fidelity, continuing His love for a thousand generations, and forgiving of wickedness, rebellion, and sin, yet not declaring the guilty guiltless, but bringing punishment for their parents' wickedness on children to the third and fourth generations.

### Lesson 1, Day Four

1.  God's plan for me is to prosper me and not to harm me, to give me a future full of hope.
2.  **Matthew 6:33** We are to seek God's kingdom and glory before our own.
    **Philippians 2:3–4** We are not to do anything out of selfish ambition or vain conceit. We're to consider others better than we are. We're to look to the interests of others.
3.  **Proverbs 3:5–6** We need to trust in God and not rely too much on our own understanding. We need to acknowledge His ways (His plan) and pursue them. When we do this, He'll direct our paths and make them straight.
    **Proverbs 28:26** Those who trust in themselves are fools, but those who walk in wisdom are safe.
    **Isaiah 43:1** We don't need to fear because we are redeemed by God. He has summoned us by name—personally. We belong to Him.
4.  Answers will vary.

### Lesson 2, Day One

1.  **A.** We are to follow Jesus. This means imitating and obeying Him. In the words of the Blessed Mother, "Do whatever He tells you" (John 2:5). Jesus' example and instructions are meant to lead us safely through this life, and into His loving presence for all eternity.
    **B.** We can know what is true. All knowledge and all mysteries are held in Christ. Because He is the source of truth and is willing to share it with me, I can know the workings of the universe. I can know the longings of the human heart. I don't have to figure out and define my own version of truth. I can trust that He knows all things and will faithfully reveal to me whatever I need to know for my present circumstances.
    **C.** In Christ, we can hope for and expect to experience "fullness of life." Isn't this what we all long for? If we want to be fully alive, tasting life in all its depth, breadth, and height, we need to be connected to the source of life, Jesus.
2.  Answers will vary.

### Lesson 2, Day Two

1.  **Luke 17:25 (fulfillment of Isaiah 53:3)** Jesus was despised and rejected.
    **2 Corinthians 5:21 (fulfillment of Isaiah 53:4–5)** Jesus bore the punishment that was due us so that we could be whole.
    **Mark 15:4–5, Luke 23:8–9, John 1:29 (fulfillment of Isaiah 53:7)** Jesus was silent before His accusers. He was the lamb sacrificed in our place to take away the sins of the world.
2.  **Matthew 1:22–23** As prophesied, Mary bore a son who was God in the flesh—Emmanuel.
    **Matthew 2:1** As prophesied, Jesus was born in Bethlehem.

### Lesson 2, Day Three

1.  The name Jesus means "God saves." His name expresses His identity and mission "because he will save his people from their sins" (Matthew 1:21).
2.  No. We all have sinned. If we claim that we are without sin, we are deceiving ourselves.
    Answers will vary.
    The wages, or consequence, of sin is death.
3.  The solution God offered for our hopeless situation was to have Jesus die for our sins, in our place. He did this for us when we were still sinners. He doesn't wait until we're cleaned up and "worthy" before we can accept this gift from Him. He offers it to us when we are helpless.
4.  Love was the motivation. God loved the world (and that means each one of us) so much that He gave His only Son so that we wouldn't perish and be separated from Him. Instead, we can have eternal life.

**Lesson 2, Day Four**

1. **Colossians 1:15** Jesus is the exact representation of God and reveals God to us. If we want to know what God is like, we need only look at Jesus. Jesus is God made visible.

   **Colossians 1:16** Everything in all of creation was created through Jesus and for Jesus.

   **Colossians 1:17** Jesus sustains everything in the world. He holds it all together and keeps creation from spiraling into chaos. We live and breathe because He chooses to sustain us.

   **Colossians 1:18** Jesus is the head of the Church. He is the firstborn of all of us who will be resurrected to new, eternal life after we experience earthly death. Jesus is to have first place in all things, most of all in our thoughts and hearts. The alternative is giving Him a little corner of our hearts. But if we make this choice, we'll never make room for the fullness of His grace.

   **Colossians 1:19** While Christ is fully human, He is also fully divine. He is not half-human, half-divine.

2. **John 1:2–3** Jesus was there at the beginning. Everything was created through Him. Without Him, nothing was created.

   **John 1:14** Jesus became flesh and came to live on earth, revealing the glory of God as His only Son. He was full of grace and truth.

   **John 1:18** No one has ever seen God, but Jesus revealed Him when He came to earth. Jesus is now at the Father's side.

3. When the title Lord is used in Scripture, it's referring to God's sovereignty (His supreme power and authority). Jesus referred to Himself by this title and revealed that it was fitting by proving to be more powerful than nature, demons, sin, and death.

**Lesson 3, Day One**

1. Personal reflection.
2. Answers will vary.
3. God will never leave you alone. There is nowhere you can go to escape His loving presence. He is with you right now.
4. God's love for you is everlasting, steadfast, and faithful.

**Lesson 3, Day Two**

1. Answers will vary.
2. **Jeremiah 29:13** We are promised in Scripture that if we seek God, we will find Him, as long as we seek Him with our whole hearts. All too often, we want Him, but not as much as we want other things. This verse encourages us to purify our motives and to long to know God more than we long for anything else.

   **Proverbs 3:5–6** As we choose to trust in Christ instead of ourselves, our relationship with Him will deepen and grow. This process isn't easy. A leap of faith always involves risk, and we tend to prefer being in control. But as we acknowledge that God's ways are better than ours, we'll grow in intimacy with Him.

   **John 14:23** If we love Jesus, we'll obey Him. As we take the time to figure out what He asks of us, we get to know Him better. When we prove to be faithfully obedient in little things, He'll reveal bigger things to us and, most important, more about who He is.

3. Answers will vary.

**Lesson 3, Day Three**

1. **A.** If we are Jesus' friends, we'll do what He commands.
   **B.** Love God. Love people. It's that simple, and that hard.
2. If we are going to come after Jesus (and this is what He requires of His friends), then we have to deny ourselves, take up our cross daily, and follow Him.

**3.** Answers will vary.

**Lesson 3, Day Four**

1. Heaven is described as the heavenly Father's house, which has many rooms. Jesus has gone ahead of us there to prepare a place for us. He's going to come back and take us to Himself, so that we can be where He is.
2. We are to believe in Jesus Christ to have eternal life. This belief is more than a cerebral agreement as to His existence. It's believing that He is who He said He is. It's a belief that requires action. We need to listen to Jesus' words, believe they are true, and live according to those beliefs. The alternative to receiving eternal life is receiving eternal condemnation.
3. Answers will vary.

**Lesson 4, Day One**

1. Answers will vary.
2. We often consider our feelings to be just as important as our reasoning, but if we allow ourselves to be led by our emotions, we'll rarely pray. God wants to know how we are feeling in prayer. In that sense, feelings are very important. He wants a relationship with the real you—not some inauthentic version of you. But when we let our feelings guide our decisions, we'll take the easy way out far too often, and miss out on being transformed into the women God created us to be.
3. According to CCC 572, prayer is a battle because we are fighting against ourselves, our surroundings, and the Tempter (Satan). Satan is doing all he can to keep us from praying. As easy as it is to give up, it's worth it to persevere in prayer because "we live as we pray." Nothing will transform us the way prayer does. Prayer increases our trust in God.

**Lesson 4, Day Two**

1. **A.** Jesus tells us that unless we turn and become like little children, we won't enter heaven. He values childlike dependence, not self-sufficiency that lives as if He is an add-on or someone who is nice to have around for the holidays.
   **B.** They talk without pretense. What you see is what you get; they haven't yet learned to live behind a mask. They ask for the moon without worrying how hard it would be for you to deliver it. They trust that you are more powerful than they are, and worth running to when they are scared. They believe you can make it all better, just by your presence.
2. These teachings on prayer highlight the importance of persistence. Children ask, and ask, and ask. Luke 11:5–8 encourages us to be steadfast and persistent in our prayer.
3. Answers will vary.

**Lesson 4, Day Three**

1. **John 3:16** He gave His only Son so we could be saved.
   **Ephesians 1:7** He gave us redemption through Christ's blood; He gave us forgiveness for our sins.
   **Ephesians 1:13** He gave us the Holy Spirit.
   **1 Peter 1:3–4** He gave us a new birth to a living hope through Jesus' Resurrection and an inheritance that is being kept for us in heaven.
2. Answers will vary.

**Lesson 4, Day Four**

1. God can do absolutely anything. Nothing is impossible for Him. This verse suggests that our prayers should be bold, and that tame, hesitant, doubt-filled prayers might make Jesus think we are lacking faith in His ability and power.

2. Jesus boldly asked God to come up with a different plan instead of the cross. He didn't hold back or hesitate. He begged God for a way out. But even as He honestly shared what He was feeling with God, He surrendered completely to God's will.

3. We do not have the mind of God. His ways are better and beyond our own. His wisdom surpasses ours. He can see into the future; we cannot. We can imagine how life would be if He answered our prayers in a certain way, but He can see how answering them would impact other people and other unforeseen events in our lives.

**Lesson 5, Day One**

1. According to CCC 685, "the Holy Spirit is one of the persons of the Holy Trinity, consubstantial with the Father and the Son." He is of the same substance or essence as God the Father and Jesus. He is worshipped and glorified with them. He is equal to them. He is fully divine.

2. A mighty wind was sweeping over the waters.
   **Ezekiel 36:26–27** They were told that they were going to be given new hearts, and God's Spirit was to be *put inside them*. This Spirit would help them to do all the things God had been asking of them, to help them keep His laws. This was mind-blowing stuff; it was unheard of.
   **Joel 3:1–2, NAB** They were told that God's Spirit was going to be poured out on them—not just the super religious and powerful, but even the women and the servants would experience it. At a time when women and servants were considered property, this was incredible. This outpouring of the Holy Spirit would cause them to prophesy, dream supernatural dreams, and see visions. What an unimaginable manifestation of God's presence and power.

**Lesson 5, Day Two**

1. **Luke 1:15** John the Baptist was filled with the Holy Spirit even when he was within his mother's womb.
   **Luke 1:34–35** The Holy Spirit came upon Mary, the Blessed Mother, and she conceived Jesus.
   **Luke 3:21–22** The Holy Spirit descended on Jesus at His baptism and anointed Him.

2. Underlined phrases: comprehends the thoughts of God, reveals God, makes known to us Christ, has spoken through the prophets, makes us hear the Father's Word, reveals the Word to us, disposes us to welcome him in faith, "unveils" Christ to us, dwells with them.
   Circled phrases: does not speak of himself, we do not hear the Spirit himself, will not speak on his own, divine self-effacement.

3. **John the Baptist: John 3:30** John said of Jesus, "He must increase, I must decrease."
   **Mary, the Blessed Mother: Luke 1:47–48** The Blessed Mother described herself as a lowly handmaid of the Lord.
   **Jesus: Philippians 2:6–8** Jesus didn't grasp at His equality with God. He emptied Himself, and became a slave. He humbled Himself, even to the point of dying in our place for sins He didn't commit.
   Humility.

4. Answers will vary.

**Lesson 5, Day Three**

1. He could speak a new language (Acts 2:4–12), he spoke with boldness (Acts 2:14–39), and his words had power and led people to repentance.

2. He told them to repent and be baptized, and they'd receive the gift of the Holy Spirit.
3. The promise was made to all the people in Jerusalem whom Peter was addressing and their descendants, and to all those far off, whomever God calls.
4. Answers will vary.

**Lesson 5, Day Four**
1. When the Holy Spirit took up residence inside me, He brought along love, joy, peace, patience, kindness, goodness, faithfulness, gentleness, and self-control. This means that I always have these good character qualities at my disposal. If I'm not feeling patient, I can ask the Holy Spirit to be patient *in me*, to replace my impatience with His presence—with His patience.
2. I don't have to pray perfectly. I can just talk to God as I would a friend, and ask the Holy Spirit to intercede for me, communicating within the Trinity in a way that I don't understand, but in a way that asks perfectly for what I truly need.
3. When I am heading into a conversation and I'm not sure what to say, or I'm aware of how important it is that my words be the right ones, the Holy Spirit is willing to *speak through me*. I just need to ask Him. I can pray, "Give me the right words! Please speak through me. Please keep me from saying the wrong thing," and He will do it.
4. I am never alone. If I need to be comforted, encouraged, or strengthened, the Holy Spirit is always there, just waiting to be asked for help. He's the quiet guest of my heart.

**Lesson 6, Day One**
1. Conversion is the first work of the grace of the Holy Spirit. It is grace that moves man to turn toward God and away from sin.
2. Justification is not only the remission of sins but also the sanctification and renewal of the interior man. Justification *detaches man from sin*. It purifies his heart of sin. It reconciles man with God. It frees him from the enslavement to sin. Justification heals.
3. We are saved through the bath of rebirth and renewal by the Holy Spirit. The bath of rebirth is baptism. He poured out the Holy Spirit on us so we could be justified by His grace and become heirs in hopes of eternal life.
4. As we saw in question 3, according to Titus 3:4–7, we need to experience rebirth and renewal by the Holy Spirit (baptism) to experience all the benefits of justification. We read in CCC 1991 that we also need to accept "God's righteousness through faith in Jesus Christ." This is what we do when we "make our faith our own." We receive God's grace in baptism. But many of us walked away from Him at some point, and are trying to find our way back to Him. This is why we need to experience conversion of heart, a true turning back to God. We ask Him to pour His faith, hope, and love into our hearts. We ask for Him to fill us. We recognize that it's God's righteousness that we need, because our own just isn't enough.

**Lesson 6, Day Two**
1. We cannot earn the grace of salvation. It is a gift from God.
2. Our salvation (justification) comes at an enormous cost: Christ's life. "Justification has been merited for us by the Passion of Christ . . ." (CCC 1992).
3. The charity (or love) of Christ *in us* is the source of all our merits before God. Grace is what unites us to Christ in love. It ensures that our acts have supernatural impact and value.
4. Perhaps we simply have difficulty with the concept of something being given that is truly undeserved. Even as we accept Christ's forgiveness and gift of salvation, we remain aware of the things we have done that were good. Our tendency to self-justify and feel a little superior to others is strong. At the same time, we're quick to attribute ill motive to others and to notice when we think they don't deserve mercy or help. This is what Jesus was talking about when He

asked, "How can you say to your brother, 'Brother, let me take the speck out of your eye,' when you yourself fail to see the plank in your own eye?" (Luke 6:42).

## Lesson 6, Day Three

1. Sin is not to have power over us because we are not under the law but under grace.
2. The law was given so that every mouth would be silenced and the whole world stands accountable to God. We become conscious of our own sin through the law.
3. The new law is the grace of the Holy Spirit.
4. Answers will vary for the first two questions. Lack of prayer is always an indication that we are relying on ourselves instead of on God.

## Lesson 6, Day Four

1. God told Saint Paul that His grace was sufficient for him, because God's power was made perfect in weakness.
2. We receive grace through the sacraments.
3. Saint Paul was content with the thorn in his life—not just this particular thorn but also weaknesses, insults, hardships, persecution, and constraints, because he had learned that when he was weak, he was actually strong; his dependence on the Lord unleashed God's power within him.

# NOTES

# Prayer Pages

## walking with purpose

Dear God,

Thank you for being at work in me, giving me the desire and the power to do what pleases You.[29] I'm grateful for Your guidance, and that I can trust that Your plans for me are for my good and not for harm, to give me a future and a hope.[30] Please show me the way of life–the right choices to make–so that I have the joy of being in Your presence and the pleasure of living with You forever.[31] The enemy of my soul wants to steal, kill and destroy everything good in my life. But Your purpose and plan is to give me a rich and satisfying life of abundance.[32] Help me to remember that even when my circumstances are hard, You are always at work, causing everything to come together for my good.[33] May I see myself as Your masterpiece–Your beloved daughter–created anew in Christ so that I can do the good things You planned for me long ago.[34] To You be the glory–You who are able, through Your mighty power at work in me, to accomplish infinitely more than I can ask or imagine.[35]

Amen.

---

[29] Philippians 2:13

[30] Jeremiah 29:11

[31] Psalm 16:11

[32] John 10:10

[33] Romans 8:28

[34] Ephesians 2:10

[35] Ephesians 3:20

# Prayer Requests

Date:

Date:

# Prayer Requests

Date:

Date:

# *Prayer Requests*

Date:

Date:

# Prayer Requests

Date:

Date:

# *Prayer Requests*

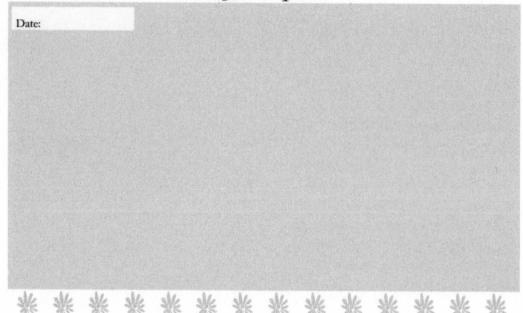

Date:

## Donation Information

Walking with Purpose expands when women in parishes respond to the inspiration of the Holy Spirit and step forward to serve their neighbors and friends through this ministry. As the ministry grows, so do the material needs of the Walking with Purpose organization. If you would like to contribute to Walking with Purpose, donations can be mailed to:

Walking with Purpose
PO Box 1552
Millersville, MD 21108

You can also donate online at www.walkingwithpurpose.com.
Walking with Purpose is a 501(c)(3) nonprofit organization.
Your gift is fully tax deductible.

*"See to it that no one misses the grace of God"* Hebrews 12:15

It's time to stop talking about how there's nothing relevant out there for Catholic women.

# IT'S TIME TO BE THE CHANGE WE WANT TO SEE.

You can bring **Walking with Purpose** to your parish!

## IT'S EASY TO DO!

### You've already got the skills needed!
- Personal commitment to Christ
- Desire to share the love of Christ
- Belief in the power of authentic, transparent community

### We'll be there every step of the way, offering:
- Training
- Mentoring
- Bible study materials
- Promotional materials

### Do you think you have too many limitations to serve in this way?

Great! That's *exactly* where God wants us to start. If we will just offer Him *what we have*, He promises to do the rest. Few things stretch and grow our faith like stepping out and asking God to work through us. Say *YES*, and get ready to watch what He can do through imperfect women who depend on Him.

Learn more about bringing **Walking with Purpose** to your parish!

Visit us at **walkingwithpurpose.com**

walking with purpose

*"For to the one who has, more will be given"*
*Matthew 13:12*

# THANK YOU

for sharing this journey with all of us at **Walking with Purpose**.
We'd love to stay connected!
We've got more encouragement and hope available for you!

## FREE valuable resources:

- Print out or download WWP Scripture Verses, can also be used as lock screens for phones.

- Join our community on Facebook, Twitter, Pinterest and Instagram for a daily boost!

- Subscribe to our Blog for regular inspiration and participate in conversations by contributing your comments!

The Walking with Purpose Bible study program is just the beginning.

Go to **walkingwithpurpose.com** to subscribe to our Blog and connect with us on Social Media

walking with purpose

# THE OPENING YOUR HEART SERIES

**Beloved:** *Opening Your Heart, Part I,* is a six-lesson Bible study that lays a strong foundation for our true identity as beloved daughters of God.

**Unshaken:** *Opening Your Heart, Part II,* is a six-lesson Bible study that fills our spiritual toolbox with exactly what we need to grow stronger in our faith.

**Steadfast:** *Opening Your Heart, Part III,* a six-lesson Bible study, unpacks why we are hustling for our worth and how to conquer our fears.

## THE KEEPING IN BALANCE SERIES

*Harmony: Keeping in Balance, Part I*
*Perspective: Keeping in Balance, Part II*
*Exhale: Keeping in Balance, Part III*

## THE DISCOVERING OUR DIGNITY SERIES

*Tapestry: Discovering Our Dignity, Part I*
*Legacy: Discovering our Dignity, Part II*
*Heritage: Discovering Our Dignity, Part III*

For more information on all Walking with Purpose Bible studies please visit us at
**walkingwithpurpose.com**

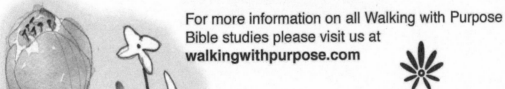

walking with purpose

# NOTES

# NOTES

NOTES